KANSAS GENEXISTENTIAL

Also by AMBER FRALEY

The Bug Diary

From Kansas, Not Dorothy

KANSAS GENEXISTENTIAL

Essays from the Heartland

Amber Fraley

Anamcara Press LLC

Published in 2023 by Anamcara Press LLC
Author © 2023 by Amber Fraley
Cover image and illustrations by Lana Grove
Book design by Maureen Carroll
Chaparal Pro, PT Sans, Franklin Gothic
Printed in the United States of America.

Book description: Discover the transformative power of friendship, the hidden depths of Kansas, and the resilience of Generation X in this humorous and thought-provoking collection of essays

All rights reserved. No part of this publication may be reproduced, distributed, or transmitted in any form or by any means, including photocopying, recording, or other electronic or mechanical methods, without the prior written permission of the publisher, except in the case of brief quotations embodied in critical reviews and certain other noncommercial uses permitted by copyright law. For permission requests, write to the publisher, addressed "Attention: Permissions Coordinator," at the address below.

ANAMCARA PRESS LLC
P.O. Box 442072, Lawrence, KS 66044
https://anamcara-press.com

Ordering Information:
Quantity sales. Special discounts are available on quantity purchases by corporations, associations, and others. For details, contact the publisher at the address above. Orders by U.S. trade bookstores and wholesalers. Please contact Ingram Distribution.

ISBN-13: Kansas GenExistential, 978-1-960462-11-4 (Paperback)
ISBN-13: Kansas GenExistential, 978-1-960462-13-8 (EBook)
ISBN-13: Kansas GenExistential, 978-1-960462-12-1 (Hardcover)
HUM003000 HUMOR / Form / Essays
HUM024000 HUMOR / Topic / LGBTQ+
BIO022000 BIOGRAPHY & AUTOBIOGRAPHY Women
HUM012000 HUMOR / Topic / Men, Women & Relationships
HUM006000 HUMOR / Topic / Politics

Library of Congress Control Number: 2023939486

This book is dedicated to all my funny, wacky, supportive, dear, dear friends and family. Thank you for putting up with me and all my bullshittery. You keep me grounded and sane. Most of all this book is dedicated to my husband and daughter, who love me for who I am despite my shortcomings and support my writing endeavors. I love you!

Abortion "is something central to a woman's life, to her dignity. It's a decision that she must make for herself. And when government controls that decision for her, she's being treated as less than a fully adult human responsible for her own choices."
—*Ruth Bader Ginsburg*

"Dearly beloved, we are gathered here today to get through this thing called life."
—*Prince*

"Toto, I've got a feeling we're not in Kansas anymore."
—*Dorothy Gale*

Contents

Foreword 1
PART I 3
1. Michael 5
2. Donella & Carol 14
3. Making Peace with the Wizard of Oz as a Kansan 18
4. The Barn of My Dreams 22
5. We Fell in Love in a Psycho Grocery Store 26
6. Adventures in K-weed 33
7. Hot, Hot, Yoga 38
8. Learning to Embrace My Turkey Neck 44
9. The Things We Used to Throw Over the Fence 46
10. The John Who Was Publicly Shamed and the Women Who Came to His Defense 50
11. Gen X Will Not Go Quietly 53
12. I'm from Venus; My Dad is From Uranus 56
13. How to Win at Menopause 61
14. Life, Love, and Lessons in Llamas 65
15. The Reason I Support Trans Folks 69
PART II 73
16. The Penis to God is in Chicago 75
17. Letters from the Kansas Abortion Wars 77
Author's Note 127
About the Author 129

Foreword

I grew up the template Gen Xer—divorced parents, key on a dirty cotton string around my neck so I could let myself in after school. In fact, one afternoon while I was walking home a man pulled up next to me in his small, Japanese car to mumble for directions. When I moved closer because I couldn't hear him, I was shocked to see he had his erect penis in his hand. (So much for the good old days.)

When I was 13 and my brother 10, our Mom said to us one Sunday afternoon: "I'm done doing your laundry. You'd better come over here so I can teach you how to do it." She also taught me to cook by insisting I help with meal preparation, which has proven to be an invaluable skill over the years. By the time I left home for college, I pretty much knew how to take care of myself and live on my own, and what I didn't know, I wasn't afraid to learn.

I'm not saying any of this because I think my generation is any better or worse than any other. But Gen X really is its own slice of uniqueness, mostly because the Eighties—which were our formative years—were so odd.

The country had come through two decades of Civil Rights movements and a terrible, divisive war that wounded the national pride. I think white America, especially, wanted to get back to peace and order and the business of America, which consists of two things: Selling crap and making money.

That was the Eighties. The Age of Excess. The age of the latest thing we all had to buy: Cabbage Patch Dolls, Rubik's cubes, Atari 2600s, Air Jordans, etc., etc. and of course, lots of hair spray.

My generation was born in an analog world and watched the birth of the digital age. We started out with board games and transitioned to video games. When we were little kids there were three television channels, and by the time we were in middle or high school, there were 100 channels, including the channel that not only defined the Eighties, but babysat a lot of Gen Xers after school until our parent(s) got home: MTV. Our music went from vinyl to cassette tapes to CDs in a single decade. We spent our early childhoods outdoors on our bikes and our late childhoods at the mall. We all learned to drive at the age of 16.

We did all of this consuming under the constant, vague threat of nuclear annihilation that loomed in the background, but at least there wasn't the parade of dead soldiers on the evening news. Just a "cold war" in which the country didn't have to do anything except spend billions and billions of dollars on thermonuclear bombs. The Age of Excess indeed.

The early 1980s saw the emergence of a mysterious, frightening new disease first named GRID by the medical community, which stood for "Gay-Related Immune Deficiency," but soon became known as AIDS (Acquired Immune Deficiency Syndrome) and eventually HIV, once doctors were able to manage the disease and it was no longer a death sentence. At the time, my friends and I were in elementary and then middle school, and woefully ignorant of the mass deaths of gay men across America—I mean, we heard about it on the news, but we didn't fully comprehend the horror.

Still, the AIDS epidemic would come to shape our formative sex lives as the use of condoms was drilled into our heads by a massive PSA campaign that didn't start until the late 1980s because up until then, there was a ban on condom advertising, both print and television. The first newspaper and magazine condom ads didn't start until 1987, and the first television ad for condoms didn't run until 1991.

The soundtrack for all this madness was a sublime mix of new wave, hair metal, hip hop, synthpop, alternative, R&B and punk.

It's this peculiar mix of influences I believe that led to my generation's motto: Whatever.

Meaning we'll deal with whatever life throws at us, good, bad, and crazy, because that's just how the world is. Life sucks and then you die, so don't have a cow, man. To my fellow GenXers out there, I see you, and I raise my fist in solidarity. Because in the end, each one of us is a brain, and an athlete, and a basket case, a princess, and a criminal.

PART I

Essays From The Heartland

Michael

Entering my fourth-grade year was a daunting experience. My parents had recently divorced, and I'd already been forced to change schools once, which was traumatic enough. Now I was expected to start again at a new school, with new kids, new teachers, and new rules.

I decided to adopt a different strategy at this school than the one before—at that school I'd been terrified and didn't really make friends. I was determined not to let that happen again.

There were two kids in my new class who caught my attention immediately—one was a wickedly smart blonde girl everyone seemed to like, and the other was a bubbly, cute, boy who was animated, hilarious, and frequently in trouble for talking too much. Those two, I decided, were the kids I wanted to be friends with.

Though it was a socially strategic move on my part, it turned out to be one of the best decisions of my life, right up there with marrying my husband.

The only way I knew to ingratiate myself to them was to be funny, and it was easy because they were both hilarious as well. I don't know if Donella and Michael remember our meeting or not, but I was desperate to earn their friendship. Thankfully, the two of them seemed to like me too, and they saved me that year from loneliness and despair, a heavy burden for a nine-year-old. I wish I could say I've been as equally a reciprocal friend to them over the years, but the truth is I haven't. Thankfully, I've managed to pull my head out of my ass, and they still love me, despite all my shortcomings.

Michael's desk was in the middle of the classroom, where Mrs. Richter could keep an eye on him. She didn't dislike Michael—quite the contrary. Her fondness for him was evident. Still, he had trouble not chatting or making the people around him laugh, and that was a party I desperately wanted to be part of.

He was a fascinating character with a penchant for fashion, even at age nine. He wore Jordache jeans, Nike shoes, and one of those satin snap-up sports jackets with bands around the collars and cuffs that were all the rage in the early 1980s. "I'm a fox," he'd declare over his shoulder, before sauntering off, a gaggle of giggling kids—mostly girls—following in his fashionable wake.

The exciting thing about hanging with Michael was you didn't know what might happen next. He was loud and silly, with a flair for the dramatic. Out on the playground, he was good at everything—he could skip rope, play soccer, swing the highest on the swings and jump off at the apex, landing like a gymnast before sprinting off across the playground, me huffing and puffing in his dust, just trying to keep up.

He was a speedskating champion and roller-skating expert. Sometimes our elementary school would host skate parties and Michael would talk me into going, even though I could barely clunk my way around the rink in heavy, rented skates that had once been white but had become a dirty taupe. Michael, on the other hand, would fly around the rink in his expensive black skates with neon detailing, weaving in and out of people, sometimes whipping around to skate backward, his feet floating across the wooden floor as Diana Ross's *Upside Down* or Queen's *Another One Bites the Dust* thumped over the sound system.

When it was limbo time, he'd skate over to me, stopping on a dime.

"What kind of pop do you want?" He'd ask in a sort of sing-song voice with the utmost confidence because the limbo prize was a free fountain drink and he was positive he'd win, because he always did. When the limbo bar was just six inches from the floor and all the other kids had been eliminated, Michael could squeak underneath by doing an extreme side lunge and flattening his upper body a hair's breadth above the floor. He'd sort of scooch underneath the bar by wiggling the extended foot while everyone watched with bated breath as he inevitably succeeded.

I'm not sure why he always gave me his pop, but it was a pattern that repeated itself over the years—I was always broke because we were poor, and Michael always made sure to supplement my finances, so I'd be included on our outings. In fact, Michael and I became besties and began spending all our time at school together, at recess, at lunch, and during class, we were either in trouble for talking or passing notes.

Mrs. Richter never said it to us directly, but she was troubled by our relationship, and she told our parents as much at parent-teacher conferences, which my mother told me about afterward. "Mrs. Richter thinks you and Michael spend too much time together," she laughed. It was a genuine laugh. My mother loved Michael and saw nothing wrong with our friendship whatsoever.

Neither did I. The fact our teacher might have concerns surprised me, as it had never even occurred to me that it was unusual or somehow inappropriate. But a boy and a girl being best friends in grade school was suspect in the 1980s.

Somehow, the gods of chance put us in the same class the following year, and the one after that. In our fifth-grade year—again with Mrs. Richter—the Cabbage Patch Doll craze swept the country and several girls "adopted" one. I had zero desire to own a Cabbage Patch Doll. I didn't love baby dolls anyway, and the Cabbage Patch Dolls were, and are, in my opinion, particularly ugly. Besides, even if I'd wanted one, I knew neither of my parents would get it for me. They were too expensive, and too difficult to locate. Of course, Michael got a Cabbage Patch Doll that Christmas because he'd asked for one, and his parents rarely failed to get him what he wanted.

By the sixth grade, Michael had added a pair of grey leather pants to his wardrobe. When our teacher, Mr. Poelma, would leave the room, Michael would wait a few seconds after the door closed before shouting "Flashdance!" Then he'd place one foot on his chair seat, the other on his desktop, lean back, grab the back of his chair with one hand, and push his body up into a backbend over his desk, the other hand triumphantly in the air. He'd then begin contorting his body in wild dance moves all over his desk and chair, much to the delight of the entire class.

Our friendship rolled into junior high school and Michael seemed to take it in stride, while I struggled. I'd been a smarty-pants rockstar at my grade school. Though I didn't have any other sort of confidence in myself, one thing I knew I was good at was school. The work was easy and getting good grades made me feel good about myself, whereas everything else about me felt wrong and gross. I longed to be prettier and skinnier, which I was convinced would make me more popular, not to mention please my parents.

In junior high school, that all changed. Suddenly there were tons of kids smarter than me, and I had trouble keeping up in my regular classes, because the only advanced class I'd managed to test into was English. Even worse, I had no idea how to dress myself and in junior high school. It seemed as though everyone had become fashion conscious overnight, and somehow, I'd missed the memo. The most horrifying 1980s junior high insult was to be accused of being on welfare or purchasing one's clothes second hand, or maybe even worse, from K-Mart.

All my clothes came from K-Mart. During those years, I gave my poor mother hell for her inability to simply have more money and purchase me designer clothes. I remember keeping this frustration bottled up until I finally exploded at her with the unfairness of it all, because the teasing at school seemed unbearable at that age. I was immediately sorry when I saw the extent to which I hurt her feelings, but also felt my mother didn't understand my feelings were getting stomped on regularly. Every day I was terrified of being outed as poor and further ostracized. Being Michael's friend gave me a sort of street cred and kept me from being a total nerd. Still, junior high was nerve wracking.

Michael, of course, was always on the cutting-edge of 1980s fashion, sporting the latest looks from such stylish Towne East Square mall stores as Oaktree and Chess King and Wild Pair.

Junior high is the first time I recall seeing Michael bullied for being gay. For some reason we were both in the hall between classes, though I was behind him, several feet away. A girl walked up next to him and asked him if he was a fag. I'm ashamed to say now I didn't speak up, but I was more afraid of embarrassing him by saying anything, and he seemed to be handling himself just fine. He looked that nasty, mean little slip of a girl dead in the eye and declared, "No, I'm not." I remembered being shocked that such a pretty, tiny, girl with a blonde ponytail could be both so cruel and so bold at the same time.

Over the years, Michael would occasionally be accused of being gay and he always denied it, of course, because this was the 1980s, a time when it simply wasn't safe to be out, besides the fact it was social suicide, especially in a conservative Midwestern town. As androgynous as many 80s pop stars made themselves appear, I think most of us clueless Midwestern kids assumed they were all straight. I was so naïve I even assumed Boy George was straight. I knew gay people existed, but as far as I knew, I didn't know any.

As such, I was sometimes emotionally conflicted over my friendship with Michael. In high school, we were nearly inseparable, yet we were not boyfriend and girlfriend. Occasionally I had twinges of fondness for him that I hoped might bloom into a boyfriend-girlfriend situation—mostly because I was desperate for a boyfriend—but Michael didn't seem to be attracted to me. Then again why would he be? Nobody else seemed to be attracted to me either, as clearly, I was too fat, too ugly and didn't have the funds to dress in designer clothes.

Because Michael was interested in clothing, music, and "being seen" like lots of other kids in the Eighties, we spent a lot of Saturday afternoons at the mall—Towne East, specifically. It was much less cool to hang at Towne West.

Going to the mall was an undertaking. Phone calls had to be made. Outfits had to be planned, complete with accessories. Hair had to be coiffed to Eighties big-hair perfection. To step into the mall looking like common trash was a teenage no-no.

Michael drove me to school every single day our freshman and sophomore years of high school until my dad finally relented and bought me a Datsun 210, a generosity I knew was thanks to my stepmother, because there's no way my dad would've ever bought me a car of his own volition.

※

When we went away to college together, the year was 1990. With the exit of the Eighties, queer culture began to surge forward and come out of the closet in a big way. People began talking about "civil unions" for gay couples, because the word "marriage" in the context of gays and lesbians was just too much for some people to tolerate.

The documentary *Paris is Burning*, about drag ball culture in New York City came out. Madonna co-opted the drag ball scene and wrote the smash hit song "Vogue," which became the anthem for drag culture. Drag Queen Ru Paul burst onto the scene and was suddenly everywhere: in movies, on television, and even documentaries like *Wigstock*. The movie *To Wong Foo, Thanks for Everything! Julie Newmar* came out, and it featured three high-profile straight male movie stars playing the parts of drag queens: Wesley Snipes, Patrick Swayze, and John Leguizamo.

Michael and I went to see *Paris is Burning* at a midnight showing on our college campus, which is the best way to see a movie. Screw your namby-pamby high-tech theaters with reclining chairs and cocktail waiters. Give me a great movie with a bunch of witty, rowdy college kids who sneak in beer and know how to have a good time. Michael bought *Paris is Burning* and we watched it at home again and again and again, because we'd moved in together our sophomore year of college. We also watched Madonna's documentary of her "Blonde Ambition" tour, *Truth or Dare*, again and again. At the time, I didn't question Michael's interest in queer culture, and in fact, I was intrigued, myself.

Another important cultural phenomenon at that time was the comedy troupe Kids in the Hall, who we, and all of our friends, came to worship. Not only was troupe member Scott Thomas openly gay, he portrayed gayness in all its iterations, from the flaming Buddy Cole character to self-hating gay bro-dudes who attempted to pass as straight. In addition, none of the "straight" guys in Kids in the Hall had any fear of playing with gender or sexuality, and all of the guys joyfully played women characters without being insulting or condescending to women.

Somewhere in the middle of our sophomore year, in 1991, Michael came out of the closet. Perhaps more accurately, he burned his closet down and never looked back. Once he was out, he was out, and he wasn't shy about letting anyone know exactly who he was, no matter their reaction.

One day, at his job at a local video store, a coworker asked Michael if his multiple ear piercings and earrings made him gay.

"No, Gary," Michael replied. "The fact I suck a dick is what makes me gay."

Michael's coming out didn't exactly surprise me at that point, because several of our friends knew he was gay and said so. But I still wasn't quite sure what to think, and I'm afraid I may have been one of the people who made him stay in the closet as long as he did, because I am known for being a judgmental asshole from time to time.

But it wasn't that I was anti-gay—I was still incredibly ignorant about how his coming out might affect his life, and our friendship. Would his parents accept him? What would dating be like for him? Where would he meet other men? How would it change the way we hung out together?

As it turned out, I would come to learn the world is a far better and brighter place for having LGBTQ+ people in it, and their mistreatment was profoundly unfair and unjust.

Once we were twenty-one years old, I accompanied Michael to the gay dance clubs in Kansas City. I still went with him after I was married because I loved to dance, and the music and the vibe were always wild and fun, and I figured my husband Jim wouldn't worry about me hanging out with gay men. At first, Michael mostly haunted a club called The Edge, which was perhaps the hottest dance club—gay or straight—in KC in the early 1990s. Michael taught me about queer culture and slang, and it was like a whole, new, fabulous world was opened to me, one I had previously never even known existed—kind of like discovering Narnia or Oz. At first, I was nervous about going to clubs where most patrons were gay men—plus trans folks and the occasional lesbian—would I be an interloper in their space? But they accepted me and welcomed me as an ally.

Eventually, straight people discovered The Edge, and young, hot, rude straight women would drag their straight boyfriends to the club and then become upset drag queens and trans women were using "their" restroom. Straight women began going out to the gay night club as part of their bachelorette parties. They were the asshole tourists of Queer World, treating the locals as if they were nothing more than exotic scenery. The Edge became less friendly and felt less safe, and its doors closed permanently when someone took a shot at the building after hours and killed the lone man inside who was closing the bar. Thankfully, other gay bars survived, and sometimes I went with Michael to the Dixie Bell or the Cabaret.

The queer community in the early 1990s seemed, to me, at least, cohesive and driven and joyous, despite the AIDS crisis. They refused to give up hope, and their determination was awe-inspiring. Gay men, lesbians and trans folks stuck together and supported each other, unlike the division in the queer community today. Throughout the Nineties the Cabaret held "beer busts" every Sunday to raise money for AIDS research.

"Do you know the Cabaret has raised millions and millions of dollars for AIDS research?" Michael mentioned to me once. I can't remember the exact number, but trust me, it was big, and my mind boggled. "That's just with beer sales," he emphasized, then went on to explain most patrons wildly overpaid for their beers at the busts, all for charity.

As the Nineties chugged along, queer culture became mainstream. Everyone came to recognize the rainbow flag as a symbol of the queer community.

One of my biggest regrets in our friendship was chickening out for a minute when I received pushback from some family members—both on my side of the family as well as Jim's—after I let it be known I intended to include Michael in our wedding, standing on my side, with the bridesmaids. I caved to the pressure and told Michael I didn't think I could include him, and I wish I could take it back. Eventually I did the right thing, ignored the worried whispers and he stood with me, as he should.

My second regret is we drifted apart for a time after my daughter was born, because Michael loves kids. I felt I was disappointing him because I quit going out to the clubs with him. He probably would have been happy if I'd just invited him to some outings with my daughter, but I was sure he'd disapprove of the direction my life was taking. Also, I was absolutely overwhelmed and exhausted taking care of a newborn and then toddler, because I had no idea what I was doing, whatsoever.

The good news is, Michael and I reconnected, and it's as if no time passed at all.

After many long years of waiting, gay marriage—not civil unions--became legal in 2015. When Trump was elected, Michael and his longtime boyfriend married, worried the Trump administration might reverse the law. Clearly, their fears were founded, and I was honored to be the sole witness during the ceremony at an LGBTQ-friendly same-day wedding chapel in Missouri.

Today Michael and send text messages the way we used to pass notes in school. Michael often texts me first, as he's up and functioning before I am:

Just watched two cars back into each other in the Dillons parking lot. And it was very gratifying.

That is too funny!

Funny, but true. Both of them had pissed me off in the store, so I think that's why it was so gratifying.

Recently he drove us to a weed dispensary in Kansas City, Missouri, because weed still isn't legal in Kansas and I hate highway driving and why break a thirty-five-year tradition of him driving us on our wacky adventures? The protocol required us to sit in their waiting room until a spot opened up in the dispensary.

"We used to go to the mall," I reminded him, and we laughed together, as we have so many times before, and will again.

Donella & Carol

Last weekend was the winter formal at my daughter's high school. She and her friends are on the cusp of driving, but not quite there, so I ferried three kids to the dance—and ended up bringing home six. Only, we didn't go home right away. First we went to a fast food restaurant, where I busied myself on my phone and left the kids to hang out together without an adult looming over them. Thankfully (for my sake), the restaurant closed at midnight, and I managed to get to bed before one a.m., even after dropping off all those kids at their respective houses.

Here's the thing: I had a blast. I had a blast listening to them laugh and talk on the way to the restaurant. Because they'd just come from a dance with a DJ, I scrolled through my own dance music collection and played a few choice dance oldies from the 1980s. When they asked me to turn it up, I did, and we all sang along, loudly. I didn't mind that their language was a little salty and blue, and I laughed at their inappropriate jokes.

It's kind of silly, but I enjoy being the fun mom. Or at least, the not too terribly cringe mom. It made me wonder, though: Is it bad to live on the edge of your teen's social life like that?

Then I remembered the mom on the orbit of my troubled teenage years, and how unbelievably grateful I am to her.

※

Sometime around the age of fourteen, I distinctly remember the last time I hosted a sleepover at our house. My best friend Donella and I tried to stay up after my mother went to bed, but Mom kept coming out of her bedroom, angry, accusing us of talking too loud and slamming doors. Though it was a long time ago, I still remember it like yesterday, and I know for a fact we were doing neither. Eventually, we gave up and went to bed, the death knell of a successful sleepover. At the time, being a teenager, I was angry and ashamed and thought my mom was being an embarrassing bitch. As an adult, I recognize her behavior was part of the emotional and mental demons she was battling.

Rather than suffer the humiliation of trying to have anyone spend the night at my house, I invited myself to Donella's house at least once a month. I mean, sometimes she called and invited me over, but more often, I asked to go there, because Donella's house was a breath of fresh air compared to mine.

For one thing, their family was usually in a good mood. Not always. There were arguments, and occasionally people got a little hot under the collar and had a good-natured holler at each other, but they always made up. Mostly, Donella's house didn't have the same gloomy pall that frequently loomed over ours.

Donella was, and is, a hot firecracker of energy and wit. That has never changed. In my mind, she had it all—she was smart, and confident, and beautiful, and driven, and outspoken, and hilarious and boys practically fell dead at her feet. Donella was everything I wanted to be but could never quite attain. I both loved her and envied her, which is perhaps a dangerous combination. What ultimately drew us together, I think, was the ease with which we could be big goofy dorks together. We had a great time no matter where we were, whether we went out or stayed home. When we went out, I tried to be a good wing-woman for her, providing lighthearted entertainment while she beguiled the boys, because we both loved boys and talked about them endlessly.

We started the sleepovers in the fourth grade. When Donella's family moved to a different school district, our sleepovers were the way we maintained our friendship. It never occurred to me at the time that not only was Donella my friend, but her family effectively gave me a second home—and made myself at home I did. At Donella's house, I could open a can of Spaghetti O's and scarf it down at 11 p.m. and nobody judged me for it. At Donella's house, one could grab the jar of peanut butter and the jar of marshmallow fluff, mix up a bowl of fluffer nutter and eat it with a spoon, anytime day or night. Donella had a huge collection of Barbies and Barbie clothes because her mother scoured garage sales for them and bought them whenever she could. My mom refused to buy Barbies for me for feminist reasons, which I kind of don't blame her for. In principle, I agree Barbie represents an unattainable image that could potentially cause little girls to hate themselves and develop anorexia. On the other hand, I really like Barbies for some stupid reason and always have. I think it's all the fashionable tiny clothes and shoes.

At Donella's house, we could watch *Porky's* or *Halloween* on cable, something I wasn't allowed to do at home—except, of course, Clay and I did when Mom was out on a Friday or Saturday night. Because Donella's mom Carol was an Avon lady, there was always an endless supply of makeup and perfumes to try. At home, I wasn't allowed to touch my mother's makeup or perfume.

At Donella's house we could be loud and sing and laugh and have fun and no one yelled at us. In fact, many nights I slept over at Donella's, Carol stayed up with us. She played board games with us, watched movies and with us, and counseled us about boys.

After spending half the night up, Carol might decide she wanted to do the grocery shopping and take us with her, at one in the morning. She would bring her coupon organizer, working the double- and triple-coupon game like a master. One night I saw her turn a hundred-dollar grocery tab into a fifty dollar one.

"You whacked that fucker in half!" I exclaimed, and rather than chastise me, we howled about it all the way home.

What I think I loved most about Carol, the thing I connected with, was her wonderful inappropriateness. Carol let us push boundaries, but she never let us go over the cliff. In my own life, I struggled with depression, while living with a mom who wasn't fully functioning either. It's no exaggeration to say that if I hadn't had Donella and her mom Carol, I might've completely lost my mind.

A few times, before Donella and I had our drivers' licenses, Carol took us to "drag Douglas," the street teenagers cruise in Wichita. It was a perfect setup: Carol drove so she could keep an eye on us, while we were free to hang out the windows and yell at cute boys without doing something stupid like drinking, or smoking weed, or wrecking the car, or getting arrested.

We laughed a lot. Sometimes we laughed until we collapsed on the floor in tears. One night Carol decided we'd make big, soft, homemade pretzels. We swung thick ropes of the stretchy dough to lengthen it, making all the obligatory dick jokes. As Donella swung her pretzel penis, a piece of dough broke free, smacking me in the throat. The innuendo was too much, and we almost laughed ourselves to death.

It didn't occur to me until I was older how grateful I am, not only for Donella's friendship, but for her mother's wildly fun stability. Carol was always there for her family, fully engaged, feeding hungry stomachs, fixing boo boos, doing the laundry, and shuttling someone somewhere. She did it all with firmness, love, and always, a sense of humor. She was the engine of their whole house, up early in the morning to begin cooking and cleaning and organizing and volunteering to help others, and she didn't stop until she collapsed in bed at some point during the night.

At the time, I couldn't comprehend how young Carol was. She'd been a teenager when she gave birth to Donella, which meant that when we were sixteen, she was only thirty-two. I think she hung out with us not only because she enjoyed it, but also because she knew how wild teenagers could be—she'd lived it.

"I dropped acid once," she told us one night.

"What was it like?" I asked, knowing Carol would tell the truth.

"I looked in a mirror and saw my face melting!" That was enough to scare me out of taking LSD… for several years, anyway, and when I did try it, I only did it the one time.

It's not at all that I believe Carol was a better mom than my mom. Carol certainly wasn't perfect—no parent can be. She was just a less strict mom.

I kind of like picking up where Carol left off, being the mom that lets kids have their space and be themselves, but not so permissive as to do anything stupid like buy them alcohol or allow them to get into any real trouble. Because I did my share of partying, I would know in an instant if they were drunk or high, and I wouldn't be afraid to confront them about it.

I think there's something to be said for the fun moms out there, who keep it real while keeping kids safe.

Making Peace with the Wizard of Oz as a Kansan

My first memory of watching the *Wizard of Oz* is a brief flash of lying on our 1970s gold velvet couch, watching Dorothy's gray house get sucked up into the sepia tornado. I was lying down because I'd had a hard day of playing and I was only four. I didn't really understand the movie I was watching, but somehow, I knew it was important. "Kansas" wasn't yet a concept for me and my family was living in Tennessee at the time. That same year though, we'd move back to Kansas, the state where my parents were born—as well as four previous generations—the place from which all our people hailed.

Like the annual arrival of the Easter bunny, the special movie came to television in the spring of every year, and we never missed it, because in our house, as in many Kansas homes, it was treated as an event or a holiday. It's *Wizard of Oz* time again! Get the popcorn! I'll probably go to my grave knowing there's a commercial break after the Cowardly Lion runs and jumps through the window of the Wizard's palace, shattering the glass.

When you're from Kansas, you're far more aware of this movie in daily life than your average American. Even though ninety percent of the movie doesn't even take place in Kansas, Kansas and the *Wizard of Oz* are inextricably linked.

For one thing, it's about the only thing people know to associate with Kansas. There used to be a time many Americans knew Kansas is the largest producer of wheat in the United States, because they were familiar with the phrases "Breadbasket of America," or "Wheat State." But no one knows those sayings anymore, and lots of people from outside of Kansas seem to think Kansas grows a lot of corn. I've found many city dwellers assume anything growing in a field is "corn." However, corn is Kansas' second largest row crop, while Iowa is the top producer of corn in the US.

Sure, some people think of the Kansas City Chiefs, but the Chiefs are a Missouri team—Kansas City is one of those cities that straddles two states—and most of the fun stuff, of course, is in Missouri. (Yes, I know they are actually two cities, but around here we don't really treat them as such.)

So often, the only tangible idea of Kansas other Americans have to grab onto, is the film *The Wizard of Oz*. When you're from Kansas, and you leave Kansas, you will hear *Wizard of Oz* Comments. "How's Toto?" people ask, chuckling to themselves, as though they're the first to think of it. Or, if you're female, they'll ask "Are you Dorothy?"

It gets old. ... At least, when you're in your teens and twenties and thirties, and things like that are annoying. Now that I'm older, I've made my peace with the *Wizard of Oz*.

When I was four, and for many years thereafter, I would be completely sucked into the wonderful world of Oz, buying every second of it. Now that I'm older, I can see the backgrounds are clearly matte paintings, and every scene is obviously filmed on studio stages. But that's not how I saw it as a kid. As a kid, Oz the movie might as well have been made with high-tech computer graphics. I bought it completely. (Okay, not the shiny plastic flowers in Munchkin Land. I wasn't a total idiot.)

I watched *The Wizard of Oz* again recently, and I was struck by how good the actors are, and how fun it is to listen to their charming Mid-Atlantic accents, which is the name for that haughty, almost British accent early American actors used. (Think Cary Grant and Katherine Hepburn.)

"No haht?" Dorothy and the Cowardly Lion ask the Tinman when he tells them the tinsmith created him without a heart. "No haht," he sighs.

Lovely.

Curious, I looked up the three guys who play the Scarecrow, the Tinman and the Cowardly lion — who also play the farmhands Hunk, Hickory and Zeke, and whose real names are Ray Bolger, Jack

Haley and Bert Lahr. They were all vaudeville stage actors before transitioning to movies. Frank Morgan, who played the bumbling Wizard and shifty Professor Marvel, started out acting in the silent films of the early 1900s. So these were all people who knew their craft well and had devoted their lives to it.

I was also struck by how young Judy Garland was when she made the film, because you don't think about that kind of stuff when you're a kid. Anyone who's in a movie must necessarily be older and more important than you. But she was seventeen years old when she worked on *Wizard of Oz*. Seventeen. She's so young that her voice is young and, for lack of a better word, pure. It's clear and unadulterated, which makes it all the more heartbreaking if you know anything about her life. I won't go into the details, but Metro Goldwyn Meyer movie studio pumped her full of drugs and used every bit of that poor woman's body and soul and then threw her out like trash when she couldn't make movies anymore. She self-destructed in a pit of despair, booze and pills. She died at the age of forty-seven.

As I watched it for maybe the hundredth time with new eyes, I wondered for a moment why no one has tried to remake *Wizard of Oz*—I hope no one does—and I think it might be one movie that's simply too iconic to touch. I can't even begin to fathom a cast that could compete, talent-wise, with the original. And I don't think even CGI could recreate the magic we all conjure in ourselves when we watch the original. There's nothing out there remotely like it. There's no other movie to even compare it to. It's an institution unto itself.

Because I've watched this film my whole life and accepted it as much a part of my life's mythos as Santa Claus, there were many specifics I never really considered as a kid. But when you think about it, Oz is an unusual movie because the protagonist is a little girl. Heck, we can hardly get little girl protagonists in movies these days, but Oz came out in 1939. Not only that, but she's a little girl hero who kills the villain. I mean, sure, it's all a dream, so technically she doesn't kill the witch, but I don't think I really understood that as a kid. I thought that somehow, Dorothy's dream was real, and in fact, in the original *Oz* books by L. Frank Baum, Oz is a real place that Dorothy visits more than once.

The Wizard of Oz is so unusual, so rare, so weird, that these days, I proudly associate my state with the film. In fact, Kansas is a lot like the movie, in my opinion. Sure, we look boring and black-and-white from the outside, but there are a few fascinating gems to be found here, and even a fair amount of weirdness.

You just have to know where to look.

The Barn of My Dreams

This barn, located on Bob Billings Parkway just west of the KU campus in Lawrence, haunts my dreams and memories. Literally. About twice a year I dream about this barn, and it's always larger than life. In real life the barn is maybe forty feet high. In my dreams it's a hundred, easy. In my dreams it's as grand as a castle, imposing but welcoming.

The barn was built of Kansas limestone in the early 1900s by a man named Harold Chamney, as part of his family's dairy farm. At that time, it was one of the largest dairies in town, with ten buildings. Lawrence Journal World archives report that it once delivered milk to 300 homes and two small grocery stores. The University of Kansas purchased the property from the Chamney family in the early 1960s. Today, only the barn and the adjacent house remain, and both are home to the KU Center for Design Research, as part of the Industrial Design department.

I visited recently, and marveled at how quaint and petite it actually is—for a barn—unlike in my dreams, where it dwarfs me. But I'm sure that's because I remember the barn from the time I spent there as a child.

I grew up in this barn. From 1976 to 1991 it was home to the glassblowing program at KU, where my dad was the glassblowing professor. Back then, it was surrounded by wheat and brome fields. When I was a kid, we called it "The Barn," and it was where my dad worked. When he started the glass program at KU in 1976, I was four years old. Throughout our childhood, my brother and I spent hours there, playing, exploring and, over the years, watching hundreds of students flow in and out of the barn, learning to blow glass.

"C'mon, kids! Let's go to the barn!" My brother and I would pile into Dad's van, and we'd pull into the barn driveway, the gravel crunching under the tires.

You could hear the whine of the gas lines fueling the glass furnaces before you even entered the barn, or the "hot shop," as my dad referred to it. Often when we arrived, the barn door was rolled open, even in the middle of winter, to let the heat out. You could feel the wall of heat hit your face the second you crossed the threshold, and if you wanted the person standing next to you to hear you, you had to raise your voice over the roar of the furnaces. ... That, and whatever music was blasting from the stereo, because the students always played music. Over the years, the music changed from the Beatles, to Led Zepplin, to Journey, to Pearl Jam, and but whatever was playing was always loud.

Once the furnaces were lit in the fall, they were lit for the whole school year, and they weren't shut down until school let out in summer. Over the summer, my dad, and usually a couple of students, would dismantle at least one of the furnaces and rebuild it, since furnaces wore out after only two or three seasons. Sometimes I'd watch my dad fitting the firebricks together like a big set of Legos.

Once they were lit and running, and the batch had been mixed—batch is what glassblowers call the recipe of silica, soda ash, limestone, feldspar and metal oxides that make up glass—the furnaces glowed ominously, full of molten glass that ran almost as thin as honey at over two thousand degrees. (Yes. Two thousand.) A steel glass blowing pipe is about six feet long. Standing at the end of a blowpipe in front of a glass furnace glowing from the sheer heat hurts. The heat causes a deep burning sensation in the skin of one's face, hands and arms, but if you want to blow glass, you must endure it until you overcome it. My dad always says that either your body adjusts and gets past that sensation, or you don't become a glassblower. Glassblowers must also wear protective eyewear, because the glow of the superheated glass puts off ultraviolet and infrared radiation, and they spend a lot of time peering at their works of art on the end of the blowpipe, making sure to rotate it evenly and consistently, lest the glass drip off the end and back into the molten body from whence it came. Conversely, keeping a heated piece out in the cold air too long will cause it to crack.

Dad was always busy at the barn, assisting students, recording grades, answering phone calls, and blowing glass. In addition to the furnaces, there were two kilns, in which completed works of glass art would be placed, so they could be brought down to room temperature slowly, usually overnight, to keep them from cracking, or even exploding, because glass is never a solid. It's always liquid—even the windows in your house are liquid—it's just flowing at a glacially slow rate. Allowing a piece of hot glass to cool at room temperature creates stress because the outer layers cool and flow slower than the inner layers.

I can still picture where the workbenches sat, with their buckets of wet tools next to them. The barn had its own smell, too: A mix of silica dust and the sour note of wet apple or cherry wood. Traditionally, glassblower's tools are made from fruitwood and stored in buckets of water to keep them from being vaporized by the molten glass. Still, after several seconds of being applied to the hot glass, the surface of the tool will often heat up and temporarily burst into flame. Sometimes the glassblower ignores the flames and lets the tool smoke; other times they'll dip it back in the bucket to douse the fire.

Glassblowing is fascinating to most folks. My brother and I saw so much glassblowing we were bored to tears by it. Instead, we roamed the barn property, doing the things kids do to keep boredom at bay. We caught grasshoppers in the field out back and fed the orb weaver spiders that made their webs in the windows. The university rented the field to a local farmer, who planted brome and bailed it in the fall. Climbing the hay bales and jumping from bale to bale was also one of my and my brother's favorite pastimes.

The basement of the barn was known the "cold shop," where all of the finish-work of glassblowing took place: Grinding wheels coated in diamond dust to smooth down any sharp edges on a bowl or a goblet or a vase, as well as polishing wheels to make the glass shine. There was also a sandblasting booth where students could add frosty details to a piece of glass artwork, and the locked room my brother and I were forbidden to visit, where all the chemicals and silica were kept.

Over the years, my brother and I got to know a few of the students, but mostly, we learned the art of staying out of the way. Glassblowing is dangerous, and Dad taught us from the beginning where we could and couldn't be, and we took it to heart.

I can only imagine what the barn meant to those hundreds of students who took a class there. I'm sure that for the students who majored in glass and have successful art careers, The Barn is occasionally the setting for a memory or a dream. And I'm sure that when the Chamney family gave up the place, they occasionally dreamt of the farm their great grandfather built, the farm where they made their home and their living. I'm sure some of the design students who work on projects at the barn today, will dream about the barn long after they've graduated.

Though I'd love to own the barn—it'd make an absolutely gorgeous residence—I'm glad the university owns it, because it'll be preserved forever, where it can continue to pop up in someone's dreams.

We Fell in Love in a Psycho Grocery Store

My husband and I, like lots of couples, met while we were in college. We worked at the same small, family-run grocery store located in a disadvantaged part of our Kansas college town: Roger's Food Center. (We employees called it Roger's Fabulous Food Center! when we were joking around.) What was interesting about the place was the cast of characters, both the customers and the employees. I was hired as a checkout girl, a job I landed only after going back and bugging the manager four times. I had worked at a similar family grocery store while I was in high school, and I knew I'd learn the ropes there quickly and he'd figure that out too, if he'd only hire me. I was desperate for a job. My sophomore year of college was starting, and I needed to pay rent.

After a couple of weeks of my pestering, he did hire me, and I quickly became used to the stream of weirdos who streamed in and out of the place every day. Most of our customers were regulars, and they ranged the gamut from wonderfully bizarre to literally insane.

I spent hours at the checkout stand, putting in my time as a checkout girl. Even though scanners existed at that point, we didn't have them. I had to actually push buttons on a cash register, and weirdly, I got pretty good at it. It was the most hated job in the store, because checkers had the most facetime with customers. Some of the customers I enjoyed very much. They were sweet, or funny, or my most favorite: Really fucking odd. Then there were the angry customers, angry because they were poor and their jobs sucked and Roger's prices were often higher than they wanted to pay, because we simply didn't have enough inventory to keep prices low, but the customers were sure the store was intent on exploiting an underprivileged section of town. Now that I'm older, I feel for those people. At the time, I was kind of the snot-nosed college kid they thought I was, wondering why they couldn't just get their shit together. I judged them silently: *Why can't you just wash your filthy kids, stop drinking and get a better job?* Now I appreciate how much life can beat a person down, especially when you're poor. I can't tell you the number of our customers who paid for their groceries with the last bits of change they could scrape together from under the couch cushions and the floor of the car. Sometimes they'd bring in a whole jar of change, and we'd let customers pay that way, but our policy was the change had to be wrapped in change rolls. Luckily, we always had spare paper change wraps on hand. If business was slow, I'd help the customer separate the change, count it out, and put it in the appropriate rolls. If I was busy with other customers, they had to do it themselves on the counter of an empty checkout lane.

If you worked at Roger's long enough, most of the regulars would eventually come to trust you, even though they were suspicious of the university and they hated college kids. Most of us working there were college kids.

There was Miss Alberta Mae Sargent who never failed to sign her name as such on her check, and would proudly tell you she was a spinster who still lived in the very house in North Lawrence where she was born.

There was Pat Patterson, the Black WWII pilot who talked about himself exclusively in the third person and would regale you with stories of him having once made an emergency landing in a field just north of the store.

"Pat Patterson doesn't care for Mr. Rogers," he'd say, referring to the store's owner. "Pat Patterson flew planes in World War II."

In fact, Pat Patterson was so proud of himself, he named his daughter Patricia Patterson. Sometimes Pat Patterson and his best buddy Curtis bought pig ears from our butcher to make pig-ear sandwiches. Clarence was a hilarious older man who'd buy pig intestines to make the "Mississippi noodles," his mother had cooked him when he was a kid. "You gotta clean 'em right," he'd tell us, grinning, and we believed him.

Dick was one of our regulars who was schizophrenic. He'd been diagnosed and wasn't medicated because Dick refused to believe he was schizophrenic. He was convinced everyone heard disembodied voices all the time—It was just that the rest of us weren't admitting it. Some days the voices were unkind and bothered Dick a lot. I know this, because he usually told me as I rang up his purchases. He'd say something like, "Today the voices are really loud. They're not leaving me alone," or "The voices have been quiet lately," with an appreciative smile. The intensity of the voices often affected Dick's mood. Days when the voices were particularly insistent and negative, his face was scrunched with irritation and worry. Other times the voices were positive. Occasionally they'd go altogether silent. Once as I was ringing up his groceries, he laughed out loud.

"The voices just told a joke," he explained, grinning as I handed him his grocery bags.

I always responded to Dick's reports about the voices that plagued him. "Oh, I'm sorry," I'd say, or "That's good!" and other such inanities, because it seemed like the polite thing to do. The fact I responded at all might be why, after some months, Dick became convinced I was listening to his thoughts. When he talked about the voices at other checkout stands, I'm sure many cashiers simply ignored him.

"Can you please stop listening to my thoughts?" he'd say, as I rang up his milk. "That's really rude."

"Dick, I swear I am not listening to your thoughts." I would say this as sincerely as I could, because I didn't want him to think I had anything against him, because I didn't. I liked Dick. Would I have given anything to hear even the briefest snippet of what was going on in Dick's head? Hell yes. But he never believed I couldn't. He'd smirk and shake his head, placing his change in his wallet.

"Childish," he'd say, as he left. But he always interacted with me the next time he came in.

Dick had a questionnaire he carried with him to hand out to anyone he deemed worthy. He gave one to me once. It had questions on it like:

- Do you hear voices?
- What do your voices say?
- Do you hear my voice?

- Can you hear my thoughts?

Of course, I wish now that I'd kept it, as a small window into someone else's mind. We saw Dick years later at a neighborhood park. During the Roger's years, he drove a Volkswagen Bug circa 1960 or so. Twenty years later, he was riding a bicycle with a small trailer attached. Though he was clean and appeared to be in good shape, it seemed to Jim and me that he was homeless. He smiled at our dog as we walked by, though I don't think he recognized us from all those years ago.

Simon was another mentally ill man you might catch a glimpse of anywhere in town, as he spent his days walking from one end of town to another. For several years, he wore the same red sweatpants and red t-shirt that said "That's my Dillon's!" referring to the Kansas grocery chain. A few times, though, he wandered over the bridge into our part of town, and into our store. One evening, when my then boyfriend Jim was counting down the day's money in the customer service booth, Simon came up to ask him a question:

"Excuse me… Do you carry the canned mixed vegetables with the ancient carnivorous orchid that pops out and eats your face when you open the can?"

Without missing a beat, Jim looked up from balancing the books and replied, "No, I'm sorry. We just carry the regular canned mixed vegetables."

"Pity," Simon said, and he wandered away. One time I was working when Simon didn't make it into the store. He got stuck walking in circles, talking to himself, in the middle of an underpass just down the street. That was the thing about Simon: sometimes he was right there with you on the same plane of existence, and other times, he was in another galaxy. A customer alerted me to Simon's presence, warning he was going to get hit by a car and I called the police. The whole community knew who he was, and though various agencies tried to step in to help, Simon, like Dick, preferred to not be medicated. When he wasn't wandering around town, he was usually in jail. Word was he'd purposely provoke an arrest when the weather started to get cold so he could spend the winter months indoors. I think most people in town wished there was a better solution for Simon, but no one could quite figure out what that was.

Perhaps the most troubling customers, to me, though, were the ones who came in drunk. Especially the ones who'd driven there, and super especially the ones who had driven there with their kids. I always wanted to say or do—something—but I was a nineteen-year-old checkout girl, and some of these people were intimidating, to say the least.

There was the day that one of our regulars, Cliff, looked at me, said, "I've always wanted to rape you," and grabbed me around the waist. I broke away, shocked. He was in his late fifties, or so. I said nothing to him because I was so rattled. That wouldn't happen today. Today, I know how to stand up for myself—y'know—after getting a few more years of sexual harassment under my belt. Thankfully, my friend Julie was on duty that night. I told her what Cliff did, and the next time he came in, she yelled at him to get out and never come back.

He never did, at least not while I worked there.

One afternoon while I was up front checking, there was a thunderous explosion outside that shook the windows. When we went out to investigate, it turned out a drunk driver in a small pickup truck had hit a telephone pole near the store. He'd been barrelling along so fast the collision sheared off the pole, crushed the truck's engine, and broke both his legs. But the man was so inebriated he managed to exit the truck, cross the street and hide in some bushes for about an hour before the police found him crouching there.

One night, after I'd been promoted from checkout girl to stock-boy, I was in the back bagging ice at the ice machine when another stock boy (an actual boy) came running into the back room and picked up the phone:

"We have an armed robbery in progress at Roger's," he said, and I remember being glad he was the one to call the cops, because I would've garbled the shit out of it. I went back to bagging ice, figuring I was safe in the back room. After all, the money was up front. Meanwhile, our friend Mark was the closing manager that night, and he had a gun in his face. The rest of that night is kind of a blur, now, but I do remember several minutes after the robber had gone, and I was still bagging ice, I saw a married couple crawl out of a pile of empty cardboard boxes in the back room that hadn't yet been broken down and bailed. Somehow, I'd totally missed seeing them come in and hide.

In order to work at a place like Roger's, the employees had to be a little crazy, as well, because normal people would quit after just a few days. Our butcher was a fierce prankster. Paul would casually drop a spinal cord in your coffee or smush some ground beef in your ear. He was also fond of sneaking up behind his coworkers and dropping an empty meat pan on the floor behind them with a BANG! He made one of our managers, an older woman named Charlie, pee her pants by doing this, and it was the only time I ever saw Paul apologize for one of his pranks. But he was genuinely sorry, because underneath the hilarity, he was a sweet old guy, and we often referred to him as "Poopsie." As far as I know, I was the only employee in the store Poopsie didn't fuck with, I think because I was dating his boy, Jimmy, and he didn't want to scare me off. Jim and I kept our relationship a secret for two whole weeks, because he was an assistant manager and I was just a checkout girl. But one day, Jim went to work with hickies on his neck and we were busted.

Occasionally, we'd get something shipped to the store in dry ice, which meant the boys could make dry ice bombs in the back room. They'd put a bit of dry ice in an empty 2-liter bottle, add a little water, then place the cap back on bottle. The resulting pressure of the off gassing of the dry ice would eventually cause the bottle to explode The boom was always big enough to hear all over the store, but neither the owner, nor the general manager cared. Often they were in on the bomb-making. Sometimes the customers would blink at the noise, but we staff always acted as though we didn't hear it, and we never told them what was going on.

There was a bar in that part of town a lot of Roger's regulars frequented, called the Congo Bar. The Congo Bar was known for its rough clientele and fights. When it went out of business, it was because it burned down. The college kids who worked at Roger's were the only college kids in town who dared step foot in the Congo, and they'd tell as much when we drank there.

"You know if you were some other college kids, we'd kick your ass, right?" they'd say. And we would agree because we knew it was true.

We employees bonded over the insanity. We went out drinking after work and many of us stayed friends over the years. At least two marriages were sparked at Roger's, including Jim and mine. Over the years, I've forgotten the boredom and tediousness of checking, stocking and facing the aisles. (God I hated facing.) But I have my husband, which also brought me my child. And when we're wrinkled and gray (okay more wrinkled and grayer than we are now) we'll still be able to laugh about our crazy Roger's gang.

Adventures in K-weed

My early twenties were a dizzying conflagration of a new marriage, college, self-doubt, crappy service jobs with sketchy bosses, crash diets, and weed. But then, that was the 1990s for you. A whole decade of angst and snark and a noticeable darkening of pop culture—music, TV, movies—everything.

Movies like *Pulp Fiction* and *Trainspotting*, which critics said glamorized heroin use, dominated the box office, and "heroin chic" became a thing—it consisted of heavy black eyeliner smudged under one's eyes as though one had carefully applied one's makeup the day before and spent the time in between strung out on heroin. It was the decade of grunge, and the *X-Files*, and false memory regression therapy, and Oprah Winfrey pulling back the curtain on abuse and mental illness in America.

Though my best friends Phoebe and Michael confessed being curios about heroin after seeing *Trainspotting*, I had no desire to go anywhere near it—nor cocaine for that matter, which was also huge in the Nineties—because I was terrified I'd be one of those people who fall in love with hard drugs and become consumed by them.

Weed was just my speed, and getting together with your best friends to get baked and shoot the shit was a basic Nineties requirement, especially at our age.

We'd usually get together at Phoebe's house because nobody there cared if we smoked up, whereas neither Michael's partner nor mine appreciated our hazy habit. It was our own intimate cabal of vice where conversation could range far and wide and strange, and most importantly, hilarious. We frequently laughed until our stomachs hurt, and for me, the release was almost spiritual. There's just nothing like a good bout of laughing with your friends or family to restore the soul.

Once we'd smoked enough to be good and silly—which didn't take much—Phoebe often insisted we make a trip to the neighborhood grocery store, referred to lovingly by the locals as the "Dirty Dillons," because it was small and outdated and grubby compared with the massive, well-lit, modern supermarkets in town. I would've preferred to stay put in the safe cocoon of her house, but she'd insist, and so we'd walk over there to pick up drinks and snacks, and we were never disappointed. There were always odd characters there anyway—being blazed made the shopping experience a little... extra.

One trip a couple of high school girls followed us throughout the store, ducking behind aisles but not really bothering to hide themselves. To be fair, we were being loud and giggly and weird, because that was part of the fun of being high out in public when you're in your own fuzzy bubble of fun. To have a sneaky audience, though, made it even more surreal. As they watched, hiding behind a display of Cadbury Eggs, Michael smacked me on the butt, cupping his hand in just the right way as to cause the resulting POP to ring throughout the store. We dissolved into giggles near the cash registers, nearly incapacitated with laughter, and I like to think those girls still tell that story because we gave them a pretty good show.

Another time, as we were checking out with our snacks, the woman in front of us decided to start up a conversation.

"I'm buying this for the Renaissance festival. I'm taking my daughter tomorrow." She announced it loudly, indicating the six pack of orange Crush she was purchasing. After we paid for our snacks and left, we realized it was January, and our local Renaissance Festival takes place in October.

When Michael and his boyfriend Steve bought a place out in the country, Phoebe became obsessed with going out there to gather ditch weed—also known as K-Weed—on their land because she was convinced it could be made smokable. At the time, a quarter ounce of pot cost forty dollars, twenty dollars for an eighth, and back then, twenty bucks would buy you an entire brown paper bag full of groceries. I was making eight or nine bucks an hour at the time, so even an eighth of weed was a bit of an expense. Still, I thought of it as a sort of staycation expense—a cheap, easy way to get away without going anywhere.

Frankly, I thought Phoebe was nuts. Hemp has very low levels of THC, and everything I'd ever heard about people trying to smoke it was that it was worthless in terms of getting high.

Still, she found a small amount of ditch weed on a drive out in the county, brought it home and dried it. When we tried smoking it, the experience was exactly as I'd heard—the smoke was acrid and plentiful, and provided no high whatsoever.

"What if we boiled it down?" Phoebe mused, and again, I thought she was wasting her time, but she started looking into processing the hemp into something smokable. She was told alcohol—grain alcohol—would chemically separate the THC from the plant. After discussing the problem for a bit, we thought we had a plan to process the hemp to increase the THC level, and we weren't even chemistry majors—Phoebe and Michael were studying theater and film, while I pursued a degree in—of all things—Creative Writing.

One Saturday afternoon, I picked up Phoebe in my little Nissan and we drove out to Michael's farm. Michael joined us and we proceeded to venture out into the pasture. It was beautiful out there with wild grasses and wild sunflowers and a pond—but no hemp.

Phoebe lifted her head, inhaled deeply and breathed out a satisfied sigh. "Mmm... Do you smell that?"

"Smell what?" I said, swatting away a fly and starting to sweat.

"Weed," she said. "I smell weed." I was skeptical. I smelled nothing, and I considered myself a decent smeller.

"I'm telling you—I smell it." She said it with authority and headed in the direction of the smell, so Michael and I followed her through the waist high foliage until we came upon a small forest of hemp, the plants shaped not unlike Christmas trees, some of which were as tall as we were. They waved majestically in the wind, sticking up above the pasture grasses.

I was shocked.

"I told you!" She was triumphant.

We hadn't thought to bring any tools to hack down such impressive specimens. I think I thought they'd be small plants we'd be able to pick leaves and buds off. I was horrified when I realized Phoebe intended for us to pull up, and take, entire hemp plants. Big ones. Lots of them. And transport them back to town in the trunk of my car.

My mind whirled—were we to be pulled over on the way home, I would be the one going to jail because we were in my car. I knew if I voiced this concern, Phoebe would tell me I was being paranoid, that the chances of being pulled over were slim to none, and in general, I agreed with that point of view. Still, the chance wasn't zero, either, and if my Boy Scout of a husband had to bail me out of the county jail—well, I couldn't even think about it.

Of course, we made the trip back from the country to her house unmolested. We transferred the plants to black garbage bags and hauled them into the house. Then Phoebe retrieved a ladder to access the attic opening, and I handed them up to her a few at a time as she spread them across the rafters in the hot attic, where the plants would dry in short order.

I returned the following Saturday to assist with our experiment.

"Bring your blender," she instructed, because she didn't own one at the time.

Then we began the hours-long process of stripping the leaves off the plants and adding them to the blender, which we'd filled halfway with grain alcohol. We'd blend up the mixture to release the THC into the alcohol, and then remove the spent hemp pulp. Soon, the grain alcohol turned Kelly green, and I say this with all sincerity: It was the greenest liquid I've ever seen in my life, like a magic potion that had been brewed in the Emerald Fucking City, or maybe leprechaun piss, I don't know.

Some of it splashed onto the linoleum, and even though Phoebe wiped it up immediately, a yellow-green stain remained. The lid of the blender was similarly dyed green, but I did figure out how to remedy it before my husband Jim saw the evidence of my adolescent behavior. I don't remember anymore what finally worked to remove the green stain.

We threw the stems and spent pulp into a black trash bag, which would go out with the weekly trash. Then we poured the verdant liquid into a pot on the stove and cooked the liquid until it reduced to almost nothing, added some crumbled hemp leaves to the mixture, spread it out on cookie sheets, and finished drying the whole mess in the oven.

By the time it was all said and done, Phoebe had a gallon Ziploc bag full of quite palatable, smokable weed with a decent kick to it.

We bought a cigarette roller and rolled perfect joints by the dozens, handing them out liberally. Still, that first batch lasted us for months. Phoebe repeated the process a couple more times until she decided it was easier just to buy decent street weed than go to all that trouble.

But if you've ever wondered, yes, it is possible to get high on wild hemp. You just have to put in the work.

Hot, Hot, Yoga

For a time in the early 2000s I ran a liberal monthly rag in my hometown in Lawrence. Despite being filled with local reporting, provocative opinions, poetry, art and music, it was spectacularly unsuccessful at making money. Despite the local liberal rabble-rousers' vocal insistence they very much wanted a "progressive" alternative to the local conservative daily, they didn't seem to have much cash to pay for it. Then again, perhaps the fault was mine, and I didn't give the people what they wanted, so to speak, though I felt pulled in a thousand different directions all the time. In addition to being hardworking and earnest, our progressive community here didn't want to settle for less, and they demanded more and more coverage and more pages we couldn't really afford to provide.

Still, it was a valuable experience—I learned my sensibilities are almost all Liberal Arts and almost no Business, which is a bad combination for a publisher. I also learned I was a coward when it came to certain things—selling ads, for instance, which is the bread-and-butter of any news outlet. Writing news stories that irked the local establishment? No problem. Trying to be a real businesswoman? Somehow, I didn't have the stomach for it.

The publication did, however, have a core base of advertisers we appreciated very much. One of those advertisers was a hot yoga studio, run by one of those people whose life seems to revolve around exercise, which is fine. It's just not a lifestyle I particularly want to delve into. I do exercise, but there are a limited number of hours I'm willing to dedicate to get the benefits of feeling and looking better. In other words, I'm willing to be a little bit pillowy in exchange for not working out too hard for too long, but still feeling miles better (physically and mentally) than when I don't exercise at all.

The owner of the hot yoga studio was, to me, an intimidating woman. One of those exercise apostles who's determined to convert every slothful potato in her vicinity. I liked it when she mailed her checks in. I always braced myself when she wanted a face-to-face meeting about an advertising campaign.

"You should come exercise with us!" She'd say this with an air of enthusiasm bordering on the maniacal. She was wiry and tan, with short, silver hair, and a personality somewhere between yogi and drill sergeant. Her waist was the size of my upper thigh, and she could've kicked my ass ten times over without even mussing her hair.

Had it been any other yoga studio, I would've been thrilled to attend. I love yoga. But this was hot yoga, and I have never had a good relationship with the summer sun or the heat—even as a child —which is a shame, because I live in Kansas. It doesn't take much for me to become overheated and then dehydrated because, like my entire sweaty family on both sides, we schpritz like fountains with the least amount of effort, and the hotter it is the more we sweat. Even a short stint of gardening or walking the dog in the heat leaves me drained and with a headache that pounds away into the next day. If I don't have enough water with me to replace the deluge leaving my body, I risk passing out. It's mostly my head that sweats—yes, the whole head and face— o my hair is frequently wet in summer, and it may not be because I just got out of the shower. Frankly, it's disgusting.

But I knew I couldn't put this lady off forever. She was expecting a reciprocal business arrangement, and I also got the feeling she considered my buxomness to be a problem that needed fixing, but who knows, maybe those were my own insecurities.

One day, she cornered me. "You're coming to yoga this week," she said, arms crossed. "No excuses. We have everything here you need. You can use one of our mats. Just bring a towel, some water and yourself." It was an order. Not a request.

It just so happened that this was right at the time the yoga studio was hosting the hot yoga champion of the world. Yes, there is a hot-yoga world-champion. In order to be hot yoga champion of the world, one must transform one's body into a Davinci-like specimen of perfection. This year's world-champion of hot yoga was no exception.

He was a tiny god with taught, smooth brown skin over muscle and bone. He was my height, young and Hollywood-level good looking with a dark man-bun. He seemed to live most of his life nearly naked and shoeless in a man bikini, because yoga was his entire existence. He was the whole reason I'd been forced to show up to the yoga studio in the first place — to take photographs of his body in impossible poses no real human being could ever get into. He had the sort of body that made you want to apologize for your own. In one pose, called firefly, he held his body weight with his hands, his legs in a V around his arms, his toes pointed straight up toward the ceiling, his perfect butt several inches off the floor. I gaped in amazement as he held the pose, and he admonished me to hurry up and take the photos.

The tiny god joined the conversation, his gorgeous eyes sparkling. "Yeah, you should come this Friday! It'll be great!" I was trapped. Trapped by the tiny god and the drill sergeant. At that point, what can you do? Nothing.

I smiled and nodded my head. "Okay," I heard myself say, and I knew as soon as the words came out I would stand by them no matter what.

No matter what.

But at what cost? I wondered off and on over the next few days. Maybe it would be fine. Maybe, somehow, my lifelong battle with heat would abate itself and I would come through the experience with that sort of movie win every person deserves to have at least once in their life. Would I be able to do all the yoga poses perfectly? Obviously not, but I'd give it a damn good go, and everyone would be impressed with the fat girl who didn't completely embarrass herself at the hot yoga class. Somehow, someway, everything would work out and the day would be saved.

When I arrived for my class, I first grabbed one of their mats, which were stacked outside the yoga studio, and noted it was unusual —padded and coated in slick plastic with no slip-resistant texture to it whatsoever. It was an omen I chose to ignore.

Upon entering the studio, I was shocked and dismayed to learn the tiny god was not only in attendance, he was right up front in his tiny yogic underwear, facing us, where he'd be teaching the class. Behind him the wall was mirrored, kindly giving the room a clear view of his muscular bottom. The room was small. Two space heaters blazed away in the corners on the far wall. The floor was covered in utility carpet that looked clean, but smelled of damp sweat. The small room filled quickly and we were packed in close together. I put my hot pink mat down on the floor, claiming a spot on the edge of the room, a desperate but futile attempt to hide. I was dismayed to note every single person in the class had one specific body type: thin and muscular. Not one body deviated from this type save for mine. The mustered-up confidence I'd managed to conjure began to plummet.

This should have been a clear signal for me to listen to the little voice in my head screaming *get the fuck out of here! For the love of god just walk out, get in your car and drive home*. No. Instead, I held my head high. *I can do this* I lied to myself, all the while knowing I was lying to myself. (Life hack! When you find yourself lying to yourself, for the love of all that is holy LISTEN TO YOUR LITTLE VOICE. This is how people succumb to serial killers.)

Then the tiny god walked to the back of the tiny boxlike room with the sweaty carpet and shut the door.

The temperature in the room shot up from eighty or so degrees to the Bikram Yoga-approved purgatory of one-hundred-and-five-degrees Fahrenheit. I started with the class, attempting the poses as well as I could, despite the fact I'd only dabbled in yoga before. At the time, I didn't really understand the broad range of difficulty in various yoga disciplines that range from restorative, to meditative, to punish-your-body-into-perfection yoga. This was clearly the latter and I had no business being there.

A few minutes into the class I realized why the yoga mats were the way they were — smooth so they could wipe the sweat off. The waterfall of sweat I knew would eventually come pouring off my head came soon enough, and there was nothing I could do to stop it. My face blazed red but I didn't need to see it in the mirror because I could feel it, the heat collecting in my forehead as though someone had an iron pressed to it. Between every pose I gulped at my bottle of water that was laughably small. I began to melt on my yoga pad like a pat of butter on a griddle, sliding around in my own sweat, which puddled under my knees and elbows or hands or feet, depending on which sweaty body parts were in contact with the mat.

I can't remember now how many minutes into the class I collapsed on my mat and lie there a few moments, trying to catch my breath, praying to recover an ounce of the strength that was rapidly leaving my body. After allowing me to lie there in peace for a few seconds, the tiny god addressed me:

"Can't you get up at all?" A titter went through the class.

"No," I replied, and they laughed. Normally I would be mortified, but at that point I was so far into heat exhaustion I wasn't even offended. I was just trying to stay conscious and not slip into heat stroke. I couldn't be mad at the ultra-fit skinny people. I could only be mad at myself — I'd known how this was going to go from the outset, but I'd done it anyway. After a couple minutes I struggled to my hands and knees, but collapsed again into my puddle of warm body fluid, knowing I wouldn't be able to hold another pose both because my body was shutting down and because I was slipping around so badly. The sultry heat of moist bodies and lights and space heaters was inescapable. Yes, even the perfect body people sweated, though it was more of a sports commercial sort of glisten. Somehow I muddled my way through the rest of the class, though I don't remember much. As soon as the tiny god ended the class and opened the door I bolted, drove home, vomited, went to bed and slept for twelve solid hours.

I thought I'd escaped, but a few days later phone rang. It was the silver-haired drill sergeant.

"I expect to see you in class next week." she said. I couldn't I knew I couldn't go back.

"I threw up and slept for twelve hours," I replied.

"That's what your body needed." She sounded one-hundred-percent positive. I knew she had no idea what she was talking about, because she had no idea what it was like to live inside my body, just as I had no idea what it was like to live inside hers. (Fabulous, I should imagine.)

"I don't do well in the heat," I said, knowing she wouldn't hear me.

"That heat is natural. It is a hundred and five degrees in India where yoga originated. It's what the body needs to exercise properly."

"Okay," I said, and ended the call.

I waited a couple days to call back, praying for her voicemail to pick up. It did.

"I'm not coming back to class. I'm sorry, I just can't." I hung up before she could pick up the call and catch me. I could imagine her on the other end, listening to my message, shaking her head in disapproval.

The hot yoga studio stayed a loyal customer until our newspaper went out of business a few months later. The studio managed to stay in business for many years.

Several years later, I'd go back to yoga class. Regular temperature yoga. The teacher was a friend, and like me, middle-aged. Also like me, her body was not perfect, but yoga made her nimble and flexible and strong, and she became my shero. Her class was challenging, but she was willing to make modifications for injuries or even just stiff joints. Her classes were made up of young people and old people of varying body types, and she helped us all adjust our routine to fit our own needs and fitness levels. There was never a feeling of competition.

Still, even though My yoga instructor and I had been friends for some time, she'd never really seen me sweat. No one ever quite believes me when I try to describe it. It's something that must be seen to be believed. Even in her air-conditioned studio with an industrial-sized ceiling fan circulating, after just a few yoga moves the sweat would begin to flow down my face, my wet hands slipping on my non-slip yoga mat. In addition to a large bottle of water, I'd try to remember to bring a bandanna to wipe off sweat between poses.

"You sweat a lot," she observed one day in class.

Believe me, sister. I know.

Learning to Embrace My Turkey Neck

When I look into a mirror these days, I see my grandmothers staring back at me. Let me be clear: I see their faces. I see their wrinkles. I see their turkey necks.

This has nothing to do with their inner strength. They were both strong, capable women who worked their asses off their entire lives, doing things I can't even imagine, like canning vegetables in non-air-conditioned kitchens from hell, tending chickens, and taking care of babies without the luxury of disposable diapers. They were miles stronger than me, but their faces paid in the end. And now my face is also paying the price of time, even though my life was far easier and I grew up in the age of sunscreen.

We are a pale, pallid people, my family, totally devoid of melanin. The whitest of the white. My grandmothers both eventually ended up with skin the texture of pizza dough stretched too thin—soft, delicate, unable to keep its form, spotted with sun damage. My daughter took one of those Ancestry DNA tests, and it explains her blonde hair and alabaster skin: We are of 100% European stock, the northern and eastern parts of Europe where skin is the most pale. She is constructed from the blood of the whitest people on the face of the earth.

I knew with my genetics that, someday, my neck skin would fail me. It started when I was 40, and I'm well on my way to my full-blown turkey neck. When I was in my thirties, I was sure I'd simply pay for a surgery to get my neck skin pulled taut and stapled to the back of my head. Now I'm pretty sure I'll do no such thing. Why put my life in danger with an unnecessary, expensive surgery? Even worse, what if my surgeon screws up, and instead of looking like a woman of my age, I end up looking like some sort of squinting alien?

Nah. I'll save that money and take a trip to Colorado with my family. I will wear sunscreen, sunglasses, and a hat. I'll be identifiable only by my neck skin, flapping freely in the wind. Because like it or not, I have become a woman of a certain age, and things will only continue to go downhill from here.

I believe with all my heart that it's time to stop placing so much emphasis on women's looks and embrace the talents and skills of all women, of all ages, sizes, appearances, period, no ifs ands or buts. Still, do you ever really get used to watching your face melt down your neck? Or being able to feel those deep crags etched into what, for so many decades, used to be the smooth surface of your skin? Aging, especially for women, has so many concrete consequences on our lives. Aging tends to render women even more unseen and unheard than when we're young.

While white skin does afford many privileges, aging gracefully is not one of them. Black women's faces tend to stay gorgeous decades past those of white women, and other women of color land somewhere in between. Lighter skin is not protected from the sun's UV rays with melanin, and it's often deficient in collagen, the protein that keeps skin elastic and dewy looking.

I have no melanin. I have no collagen. Instead, I'll have the same melting, spotted dough my grandmothers had in place of where my face once was. I'll just have to take solace in the fact that I never judged my grandmothers for their turkey wattles. I loved and respected them just the same, wrinkles, neck flaps, and all.

The Things We Used to Throw Over the Fence

When we first moved into the house in which we live, the year was 2004. The housing market was in its full upswing. The house we bought hadn't even been finished being built, but it was close to the turnpike, and moving there took a full half hour off my husband Jim's commute time. Environmentally, the trade-off was probably a wash, or maybe we made things worse, I don't know. We certainly weren't polluting as much with the car, but we were contributing to urban sprawl.

When we moved into our brand new house, we didn't even have a back yard. The builder sodded out front, but it was up to us to plant grass out back. Though there were people living on one side of us, there was no house on the other side, just an empty, muddy lot littered with chunks of limestone. There were also no houses behind us, only an empty field where a farm had once stood. But we knew that would change, and quickly. As I said, the housing market was blowing up and people were buying houses faster than the contractors could build them.

When we first moved in, the wildlife was thrilling. Wild turkeys grazed in the empty field behind our house. Deer wandered through the field in the day, and strolled our neighborhood sidewalks at night, leaving their droppings as evidence in the morning. Red tailed hawks circled overhead and dove at the field, picking up snakes, mice and rabbits. Some evenings, coyotes would gather outside our back fence to chatter and howl, the noise goosebump-inducing and otherworldly. Racoons and red fox hopped in and out of the storm drains up and down the block. One day, as I washed dishes at the kitchen sink, I glanced out the window to find a bobcat staring back at me. We gazed at one other for thirty seconds or so until I moved to get a closer look. When I reached the window, she was gone.

Then the housing market crashed. Building stopped completely for a few years, then started up again, but not in the field behind our house. Neighborhoods popped up around us, though, and as more and more people moved in, the wildlife gradually moved away.

But the field behind our house stayed wild and empty, for an entire decade. Eventually they cleared the field of trees, but we still had a spectacular, unobstructed view of the river valley. Because no one was behind us, we'd throw things over the back fence into the field. Nothing toxic or dangerous. Just biodegradable things we needed to get rid of and were too lazy to dispose of in more proper fashion. When I weeded the garden, for instance, I threw the pulled weeds over the back fence. When I'd make a big pot of soup that didn't taste quite right and we just couldn't seem to finish it all, I'd dump the leftover soup on the other side of the fence. When the Halloween jack-o'-lanterns would begin to cave-in and mold, we'd heave them over the fence. Trim the rosebushes? Throw the trimmings over the fence. For ten, full, glorious years, we threw things over the back fence with abandon.

Eventually, though, when the housing market really began to pick up steam again, contractors started the process of building houses in the block behind us, the cul-de-sac asphalt having been put down a few years prior.

"I wish we could afford to buy those lots," our daughter said when the building started, and we all agreed. The three of us watched the construction progress with bitter resolve. When they started pouring the slabs for the new houses, I suggested that Oops! Maybe our dog would escape and run through the wet cement and they'd have to start over. One evening when we were standing on our back deck, contemplating the PVC pipes sticking up out of the now-dry concrete foundations that would constitute the new houses' sewage systems, my husband had a clever suggestion: "We should go drop softballs down all those pipes. Or stuff them with dog poop. That would be awesome."

"Concrete," I said. "We could mix up some fast-drying concrete tonight and pour it down all the holes." We continued to think of things we could stick down the holes until we were nearly in tears, cracking each other up.

As the houses themselves began to be constructed, the three of us would often muse out loud that it would be such a shame if "something" were to "happen" to the houses "accidentally" before anyone moved in. "Wouldn't it be terrible if those houses were to burn down?" our teenager said. "On a totally unrelated note, where can I find a lighter?"

At the end of the summer, a house went up in the lot directly behind us, and it was a shock. Construction happened quickly, and each day I eyed the changes, wondering how long it would be before the house was move-in ready. One morning I left to run some errands, the house standing there, finished, in its dirt-and-rock-strewn lot. When I came home that afternoon, the lot was carpeted in fresh green sod squares and sprinklers fanned the new lawn, watering furiously, and I realized that was it. The end of throwing things over the fence. The end of our view. The end of an era.

We've had new neighbors in the field behind us now for about a year. They seem like lovely people. I wouldn't know, because I haven't introduced myself to them. One house seems to be home to a middle-aged lesbian couple with dogs. One is home to a heterosexual couple with two small children, a boy and a girl. One is home a young lesbian couple with a baby. We have no issues with any of these people based on who they are. We don't want them there because we don't want *anyone* there.

Before, Jim and I could walk around in our bedroom naked with the curtains open because no one lived behind us. I can't go scrounge for landscaping rocks in the lots that are now their yards. When we had our fence put in, I insisted we have a gate installed in the back of our fence, because I had a feeling we'd need to have access to the field out back and I was right. Jim trimmed the weeds back there with a weed-wacker to keep them from invading our yard, and more than once I had to dash out the back gate when our dog got loose. The new neighbors probably wonder what kind of freaks we are, what with that gate to their back yard.

That's fine. They can wonder.

Now when I pull weeds, I must put the clippings in the bin for the city to haul away, which seems like a waste of gasoline. When we have leftover food that's going bad, I have to bag it and trash it, instead of dumping it over our back fence for the wildlife.

We don't like the people behind us because we just don't. We don't like them on principle. Their houses block our view and feel like a rude invasion of our private space.

Sometimes we joke about throwing things over the fence now, and we laugh like maniacs at the image of moldy jack-o'-lanterns splatting on their manicured lawns. If they only knew.

The John Who Was Publicly Shamed and the Women Who Came to His Defense

In 2019, my hometown newspaper did something weird: They posted the booking photo of a man who got busted trying to solicit sex from a grown woman. I say it was "weird," because I can't remember our hometown paper *ever* printing the face of a john arrested for soliciting sex. They'll post photos of rapists and pedophiles who are charged with a crime, and that seems fair to me.

But this guy hadn't been trying to solicit a minor. He'd spent time trying to work out a sort of monthly "sex contract" with what he believed to be a female sex worker — except it turned out to be the local cops running a sting.

His booking photos were haunting. The man looked sad. Tired. Defeated. And it made me boiling mad. Here was a man who wasn't trying to coerce or rape anybody. He was just trying to get some sex into his life, and he was willing to negotiate and pay for it. According to the accompanying news story, he was willing to pay well: Two thousand dollars a month.

I consider myself a hardcore feminist, and I was angry for this man. I was angry because instead of doing something truly horrible and non-consensual, he went searching for sex responsibly, and ended up being publicly shamed for it. The more I thought about it, the more furious I got.

So, I left a comment under the story, letting the paper know I thought it was repulsive the way they were outing this man, who, morally, hadn't done anything wrong. Above my comment, another woman had already weighed in, also defending the man. As the afternoon went by, more and more women left comments expressing their disgust that our local newspaper would humiliate one of our own citizens this way. A few men expressed their support for the man as well, but the majority of comments came from women:

- *So you're reporting on this and dragging this dude through the mud because he was willing to pay for sexual relations from another consenting adult? And why was an officer working for the Drug Unit posing as a sex worker? Then you mention his business and a quote that he is a people and family person, like that couldn't possibly be true because he wanted to have an nsa arrangement? Why go after this guy specifically? I have so many questions lol*
- *What a waste of time and taxpayer money, y'all need to be going after the PEDOPHILES that run rampant in this town. This article reads like a gossip column.*
- *This is SO GROSS. Leave this man ALONE. He wasn't soliciting a minor!*
- *For real this should be taken down. Your community is telling you they don't want this kind of scarlet letter-esque reporting from their newspaper, you should listen.*
- *bitch let this man go and give him my number*

Why were women, particularly feminists, willing to stand up for a john? Why wouldn't we want to shame a man who was soliciting a woman for sex? Because the deal the man and the sex worker had come to was not only helpful in making the sex worker a living, but it was also respectful to women in general, and women appreciate that shit. We appreciate it so much we're willing to stand up for a sad, unfairly outed and shamed man in our community whom we don't even know.

Feminists don't hate sex. Quite the opposite. We just want the act to be fair and consensual. A few women in the comment thread stood up for sex workers, too, pointing out that this kind of old-fashioned "policing" simply makes life more difficult, and dangerous, for sex workers. And that got me to thinking about why evangelicals hate prostitution and strip clubs so much: Because women can make a good living at it, and women who make a good living are independent women. No more marrying the cow and getting the milk for free. Nope. In a world where women have agency, hetero men might have to pay for sex.

The horror!

It's long past time for sex work to be decriminalized. Rather, it should be legal, but regulated for health and safety reasons. And we certainly don't need to be publicly shaming decent, good men.

Gen X Will Not Go Quietly

Author's Note: This essay was first published on my blog at Medium.com, on January 14, 2020. Some essays I toil over for days, weeks or even months, but this was one I tapped out in about fifteen minutes. It was inspired by the essay Gen X is Sick of Your Bullshit, by Mat Honant published back in 2011.

As a blog entry, this one did pretty well, with over ten thousand views by January 30. Then on January 31st, Kansas City-based, New York Times best-selling writer Jen Mann, author of People I'd Like to Punch in the Throat, shared the entry on her Facebook page and the post went viral. In a few days, over 1.5 million people read and shared it, and I ended up making about a thousand bucks for it, which is not bad for fifteen minutes' work.

This is the original version of the essay, which is still pinned to the top of my blog.

Gen X refuses to die with dignity. We will die in the spirit of Grace Jones and Poison, thank you, as we express ourselves in any way we see fit, whether that be in a suit or full body suit of tattoos.

Most of us are not, as our parents did, dressing our age. We see those articles — the ones that say we're supposed to stop wearing strappy sandals and high tops and combat boots and miniskirts and skintight jeans with holes and 'locks and tattoos — and we consider it for a second and then we say, "fuck that," because we've always worn whatever we wanted and we don't particularly give a crap if you don't like it. We grew up in the 80s, the age of flash and color and punk and metal and hip-hop and we learned to live loud and we aren't giving it up. Our music is still loud and so are our clothes. So are our opinions, which we're not afraid to share with you. We might be leading the PTA or playing bass in this cool little band on the side, or maybe we're just taking our kid fishing, to show them what it's like to do something outside.

We lived through the era of Reagan and the fear of the Cold War and we saw the wall come down and we supported our LGBT friends until we helped to vote for the passage of gay marriage. We came of age in the era of androgyny (the precursor to gender-neutral), and AIDS, back when the President of the United States understood Russia was not, and likely can never be, an ally.

We have now seen most of this bullshit before, so you're not going to fool us easily. Gen X may be a small generation that's stretched too thin right now as we look after our kids and our parents, but that just makes us all the more wary and skeptical. We're not sure if the country is going to survive Trump, but we saw the country survive Reagan and Clinton and Bush II, so we suspect there will something afterward, whether the dust settles after one or (God forbid) two terms.

We like to listen to Lizzo and Duran Duran and Tupac and The Cure and old Madonna and Childish Gambino. And also old country, old rock 'n' roll, old jazz and occasionally, some classical. We grew up on tacos and pizza and burgers and learned to love sushi and bulgogi. One of our kids is having gender identity issues and we're trying to figure out how to help our partner adequately care for their parents, while making sure our own parents get to their doctors appointments. We're tired. But we still like to go out and have a drink once in a while and maybe even sing a little karaoke.

We're not satisfied to stay in a marriage that isn't working, we'll divorce responsibly, making sure the kids' concerns take center stage, because that's probably not what happened when our parents divorced.

We know how to cook dinner, secure a mortgage, air up a bicycle tire and skateboard, though we don't get on the skateboard much anymore. We do yoga, though, when we can.

And as we get older and wrinklier and our hair whitens and we're stooped over barely shuffling along, we might have to switch to orthopedic shoes from our Chucks (if we haven't already), but we'll still have Guns N' Roses blasting into our hearing aids, dammit. You can just go ahead and play Prince at all our funerals.

I'm from Venus;
My Dad is From Uranus

My dad and I, like so many Americans today, are living out the philosophical divide plaguing this country. I am a libtard. He is a libertarian. I am a feminist. He is most decidedly not. We are both white. My dad, about 20 years ago, became an investor in a strip club in Missouri. For the record, I don't have a problem with that. I'm pro sex worker and this is a free country. A woman should be free to make money in whatever manner suits her life, and a man should be able to own a fifteen percent share in a strip club if he so desires. I'm certainly no prude, and I'm all for freedom and bodily autonomy.

God bless America.

From the beginning, the strip club was popular and successful, catering to the Army base nearby. But after a few years, a new governor decided to wage war against the state's exotic dance industry. When the laws changed to require that exotic dancers wear pasties and thongs — or clubs had to cease serving alcohol — business dropped off and the club struggled to stay open.

But this is America, and like all good capitalists, my dad's business partners opted to make lemonade out of a lemon situation. In the area surrounding the strip club, right off fabled Route 66, they founded the fake town of Uranus, Missouri which, to this day, is a fun little unincorporated tourist stop. They opened a tattoo parlor and a restaurant next to the strip club. But what really transformed Uranus into a tourist sensation was the eventual closure of the strip club, and the addition of a fudge shop: The Uranus Fudge Factory, which catapulted Uranus into family-friendly marketability. Their tagline is The Best Fudge Comes from Uranus.

Almost immediately, the fudge shop became ridiculously lucrative. Soon they added a firing range, a sporting goods store, a sideshow museum of oddities, an axe-throwing facility, and a rocket. The whole complex bills itself as an all-American, rootin-tootin' genuine roadside Missouri experience. When they purchased the rocket, they also launched a weekly newspaper — the *Uranus Examiner* — so they could run the headline "Mayor Lands Rocket in Uranus." For a brief time, the *Examiner* published actual local news, until prominent community members convinced area businesses to not advertise with the paper, saying a newspaper with such an indelicate name would make the area a laughingstock. After just a few issues, the *Examiner* ceased publication.

"It was only because of the name," Dad grumbled. I was struck by the fact he didn't get too angry about it, because the people who were against him vote the way he does. If it had been libtards who shut down his newspaper, there would've been hell to pay.

Now that Uranus, Missouri, is booming, my dad is reveling in the very American investor checks he's receiving. He loves to call me every couple of weeks and give me the rundown on what's up in Uranus. According to him, everything in Uranus is the "biggest" and the "best."

He says things like, "Our restaurant serves the biggest chicken wings you can buy," and, "We make the best fudge in the country." In addition to good family fun, the tourist trap sells an insane number of t-shirts, mugs, and other merchandise that features endless fudge-and-butt jokes which uptight libtards might consider a little homophobic, but real Americans know to be hilarious. Things like *Uranus Fudge Packer's Union, Proudly Packing Fudge in Uranus Since 2015*. Or *Uranus Mortuary: We bury 'em deep in Uranus*.

"Guess how much fudge we sold last year," he said to me once.

"Eighteen tons," I replied, thinking my guess to be outrageous.

"Twenty-two tons," he said, delighted I had under-guessed.

I had to admit I was impressed. That's a lot of fudge.

The international tourists, my dad informs me, are crazy for Uranus. Because what's more American than guns, axes, and fudge all in the same place? For many of them, it's the first time they've ever had the chance to fire a gun, and they're thrilled to spend an hour or two in Uranus, soaking up as much Americana as they can during their visit to the 'States.

Here's the thing: I would never invest in a strip club, or a gun range, or an axe-throwing facility. (I might invest in a fudge shop.) But this is America, and that's my dad's right. As a writer, nobody loves free speech and freedom of expression more than I do. But truth be told, I'm sort of glad the strip club closed, although I feel bad for the women who had to find other work. See, the strip club was what my dad and I used to talk about — or, more accurately, he would talk and I would listen. In one of our last conversations about the club before it closed, he lamented how it seemed to him as though those beautiful women were pulling a fast one on the all-American boys who frequented the establishment.

"Sometimes I kinda feel sorry for those guys," he said, wistful, and I could hear in his voice that he identified with them. My dad has been single for many years now.

"Oh yeah?" I said, steeling myself for the follow-up.

"Yeah, I mean... some of those guys are just lonely. And sometimes I can't help but think those girls are kind of taking advantage of them."

I can't remember exactly how I replied, but I know I made the conscious choice not to provoke an argument. I probably expressed some sympathy for the men, because I can honestly see that side of things. I'm sure there are men who go into strip clubs simply because they long for human contact. Of the soldiers who frequented the club, I'm sure there were a fair number who were just scared kids shipping out for the first time, trying to distract themselves from being afraid.

I briefly thought about trying to explain that while, yes, many of those men were probably lonely, none of those women would even be dancing in that club if not for lonely men willing to pay. I wanted to point out that those women were little girls once, just like I was a little girl once, who had dreams of becoming doctors or scientists or artists. I wish I could've made him understand that a lot of those women probably used the tips they earned to support their families or pay for college. I wished there had been a way to make him understand how, when I was younger and more sensitive, it hurt that he valued women who were thin and pretty, in a way he's never valued me, because I'd never been that thin or that pretty, and never would be, no matter how hard I tried.

Of course, I never said any of those things because I know my dad. Anything I might say to try to get him to see the world from a different point of view would only cause him to become defensive and angry and unable to hear. I knew he couldn't begin to wrap his head around an experience as alien as that of being a woman, nor would he even want to make the attempt. So, I'd stay quiet, and listen to his reports after visiting the club, where he'd delight in being "Treated like a king." The bar would pour him complimentary drinks while the dancers sat on his lap, and I know how much my dad is loath to tip.

Do some women enjoy being exotic dancers? Of course they do, and there's no shame in the work. At least there shouldn't be. For some reason, while we don't seem to have a problem with men who pay for women to take their clothes off, we reserve all our disdain and judgement for the woman who chooses to supply a commodity that's always in massive demand. It seems obvious to me that this dynamic is not only profoundly unfair, but downright dangerous for all women. For many people, though, this type of thinking is natural and good, and simply the way of things.

We talk about the political divide in this country as though it's about differences in issues, such as gun control or climate change. But it's more than that. It's about how we see ourselves and each other, whether we understand that's what we're doing or not. To me, Uranus, Missouri, is a tacky farce of America, but to guys like my dad, it *is* America — the money, the guns, the candy, the naked women — all of it. Who the hell is some libtard to come along and upend his notion of what America is and what makes it great?

Which is why my dad and I, if we want to talk at all, must talk about superficial things like fudge. We won't talk about any of this country's most pressing issues in any depth because the second we do, we dig down to who we are. This divide in America isn't over issues. It's about who each of us are as individuals who expect to be treated fairly. Except we can't even agree on what "fair" is. Conceding the issues feels like conceding a part of ourselves. The way I see it, one group is tired of conceding and the other doesn't even understand what conceding looks like. Ironically, my dad sees it the exact same way, but, of course in his world, his is the side that's had to make nothing but concessions.

Thankfully, these days, instead of the strip club, I get to hear about fudge sales. And thank God we can talk about fudge, because like most of left and right America, we sure as hell can't talk about anything else.

How to Win at Menopause

Congratulations! You have reached one of the most significant stages of a cis-woman's life. Some people will try to tell you menopause is an uncomfortable nuisance that will make you feel irrelevant and less like a woman. Well… kind of. Not that menopause is always a picnic, but there are some advantages, and if you do things right and with a good attitude, you can absolutely win at menopause.

Take advantage of your invisibility

You should find that you now have the power of near invisibility. (You may have felt this coming on in the last few years, as fewer and fewer people acknowledge your presence.) You'll find that gathering with your fellow menopausal friends will magnify this effect, rendering your group all but imperceivable to everyone. Feel free to go out in public and laugh, cackle, make plans to take over the world — whatever you want — in complete obscurity.

Since no one can see you, be sure to wear what you want, do your hair the way you want and wear your makeup the way you want—or don't wear any at all. I decided to color my hair purple a few years ago, and it was one of the best decisions I've ever made, because it makes me happy and I no longer give a shit what anyone else thinks about my looks.

Use your newfound rage for good

You also now possess more power than you ever will in your entire life. See, by the time you're this age, you're pretty much over being endlessly accommodating to others. You should notice your hormones have shifted away from your younger days of being weepy and timid at certain times of the month, to raging fury at the drop of a hat. You will likely find you have zero patience for bullshit, and you won't be bothered by making a scene when your small reserves of patience are gone. So, when you let loose your temper — which you will—people will subconsciously associate you with their mother, or a particularly frightening teacher or nun. In an instant, you'll find you can go from unseen and unnoticed, to a real force to be reckoned with. Be sure to wield this new power with justice in mind: Speak up against bullies for those who are younger, weaker, or less advantaged than you. If you are a middle-aged white woman, speak out to the cops if you see them treating someone badly. Older white women are the only group of people who can mouth off to cops and get away with it (usually). It's our super power, and we should weild it accordingly.

Make no mistake — middle aged women are intimidating. We do not have time for anyone's nonsense, and we're no longer afraid.

Be prepared for sweat

I'm sure that by now, if you're not experiencing it yourself, you've heard the stories about menopause and night sweats. But wait! There's more! You may also experience coffee sweats, wine sweats, beer sweats, doing housework sweats, eating spicy food sweats, after shower sweats and sitting around doing nothing sweats. To combat this, I have taken to carrying hand fans with me everywhere, just in case. Some women prefer the battery-operated variety, but I don't care for the noise, which is too close to that of a vibrator. Besides, I like to coordinate my fans with my outfits. Don't be shy about pulling out your fan in public, either. Wield it with the confidence and dignity of a woman in church. Throw out the occasional "Amen!" if the spirit overtakes you, as you create your own breeze. No one will pay any attention, anyway.

It's also a good idea to carry hankies, bandannas and/or tissues in your pockets or purse to mop up the overflow when the sweating is really out of control. If you're a makeup wearer, carry some extra foundation for touch-ups when necessary.

Get comfortable with your body & embrace your sexuality

Once in menopause, your body will stop producing some hormones and increase production of others. One of the casualties in the hormone shift will be your skin, which will be drier, but ironically, may begin pumping out teenage levels of oil (sebum) to combat the dryness. On top of that, your skin will lose buckets of collagen, the protein that makes your skin elastic and youthful. As a result, your skin will become thinner, saggier and more wrinkled.

In addition, your body will produce more androgens ("male" hormones) and less estrogen ("female" hormones). This hormone shift may cause menopausal symptoms such as voice deepening, enlargement of the clitoris and growth of facial hair.

Learn to embrace all of this. You can't stop it, it's going to happen, so put on your granny panties and deal with it. Shave off that new beard, moisturize your face, put on your daily sunscreen and take your HRT (hormone replacement therapy) if you've opted for chemical enhancement. Top it off with your sun hat and use your deeper, more authoritative voice when someone ignores you:

"Excuse me. I believe I asked for more iced tea, please. Thank you."

Be aware that despite all these changes to your body, and your new powers of near invisibility, you have now entered the fabled cougar zone. That's right. A small subset of young people will now be inexplicably sexually attracted to you, mustache, wrinkles and all. This will include young men, young women and yes, the young gender-fluid. For whatever reason, your mature looks, combined with your newfound confidence, your huskier voice, your throbbing clit and not giving two fucks about what other people think, is a POWERFUL aphrodisiac for some young people. Proceed cautiously or with newfound sexual abandon. The choice is yours. Just be sure to stock up on lube because menopause causes vaginal dryness.

Toke up

If you choose to take some sort of hormone replacement therapy (HRTs), you'll likely find they don't relieve all your negative menopause symptoms. Once you enter menopause, you may find you have trouble sleeping through the night, and you'll probably have nagging aches and pains to deal with. But research shows that marijuana use can mediate many of the negative symptoms of menopause. It can help you sleep more soundly, help regulate those fluctuating moods, and can even help regulate those temperature swings. There are also studies that show marijuana (or CBD) consumption may help strengthen bones, which is helpful since menopause often brings on osteoporosis. Oddly, partaking of the Devil's lettuce may also help regulate your weight — while some strains can give you the munchies, studies show that people who regularly smoke have lower BMIs than people who don't.

Doing the chronic won't make you sweat like drinking wine does, and since most people can't see you once you enter menopause, they won't even dream that you're doing the pots. The cops will be busy hassling the young'uns while you and your gal pals get high out in the parking lot before your brunch to take over the world. You'll be happier, healthier, and besides, you deserve it, after all the crap you've put up with all these years being a woman.

Take these tips to heart, and you too can win at the change of life.

Vive la menopause!

Life, Love, and Lessons in Llamas

For over a decade, I've been a freelance writer for a local magazine. My editor does a great job of coming up with new and inventive story ideas and angles, and in 2018, he had one of his more inspired ideas.

"How would you like to live-Tweet the llama competition at the Douglas County Fair?" he asked.

I thought it sounded fun and interesting, but also a little intimidating. Live Tweeting an event requires quick thinking and even quicker fingers, all while trying to not to Tweet out an embarrassing typo, or worse, incorrect information. But it's become a required part of journalism, so one must evolve with the times.

The full assignment was to write a feature article for the magazine about the kids, and the llamas, of the Douglas County 4-H Llama Project to help hype the event before it happened. Interviewing the kids and writing the article ended up being a big help to me, because it allowed me to meet the kids, and their llamas, before live-Tweeting the actual competition. I learned everybody's names, their background stories, and lots of interesting llama facts I could pass on to our Twitter audience during the competition.

Two of the members of the llama project were sisters, about three years apart. The younger girl was bright and talkative, while the older sister was more soft-spoken, but they were both dead serious about 4-H. Though the family were not farmers, the girls had convinced their parents to allow them to keep several animals for fair competition, including bucket calves and pigs, all on their rural property. The older sister, whom I'll call Lizzy,* had charge of the older llama, a tall, graceful animal the color of coffee named Ferris, while the younger sister, Alice, was raising Ferris' son, Chip. Chip and the younger sister were well-suited to each other, as he was as bright, cheerful, and outgoing as his human counterpart. Chip was a cute, funny little dude, on the short side, with scraggly white hair and black spots.

The younger sister explained to me that Chip was "super chill," and that's exactly how he appeared. He was content to be near Alice and complete whatever strange tasks she trained him to do for the fair. He trusted her, and she him. His soulful llama eyes with his long, beautiful lashes belied his young age.

Ferris, on the other hand, was a nervous mother who tended to fret over son Chip. She was a good match for the older sister, who was calm and patient with Ferris, as Ferris could become a little squirrelly when stressed.

All the kids had unique relationships with their llamas, and all the llamas were fiercely loyal to their kids. Llamas are guard animals, often employed by farmers and ranchers to watch over herds of cattle and scare coyotes away. Llamas also get lonely, so most farmers and ranchers know to keep llamas in pairs, or make sure there's a horse or a donkey around to keep them company.

In interviewing the kids, they informed me the llamas recognized each other at the fairgrounds and seemed to enjoy being able to see each other for a week out of the year, a fact that was as fascinating as it was heartwarming. They also explained to me llamas are smart and easy to train, which allowed the human competitors with a penchant for procrastination to put off training their llamas until a week or so before the competition.

One of the boys competing, Clint, raised his llama, Dolly, from birth, as the family hadn't known when they'd purchased his mother that she was pregnant. Dolly's birth was a total surprise — one day Clint went out to the barn to feed Dolly's mom and there was a baby llama — known as a cria — at her feet. Clint named Dolly and helped to raise her, and Dolly had formed a tight bond with Clint. When I first met them, Dolly had to step forward and sniff me up and down before stepping back next to Clint, as if she was his personal bodyguard.

The relationship between the kids and their llamas was more

like a dog-kid relationship than your typical 4-H-kid-livestock relationship, because of course most livestock is sold at the end of the season and ends up as food. Earning ribbons with a llama takes work and a relationship built on trust.

The 4-H llama competition consists of categories such as Public Relations, Obstacle Course and Pack Course. Because llamas are increasingly being used as public service animals to cheer up hospital patients, and participate in parades and petting zoos, the Public Relations portion of the competition usually involves the kids putting a visor on their llama's heads and walking them through a curtain of streamers and allowing themselves to be petted by a volunteer from the audience, among other things. The obstacle course requires the kids to lead their llamas across tires, over a teeter-totter and through a kiddie pool. The pack course requires the llamas to navigate obstacles while also wearing a backpack, because llamas have been, and are still, used as pack animals in South America to help carry items up mountain trails.

Judges score each kid and llama's performance, and ribbons are awarded in each category. The kid and llama with the highest score at the end wins the title Champion of that year's competition.

But the piece de resistance of the llama competition is always the final category — the costume category.

Usually, the kids coordinate their own costumes with their llamas: one year Clint and Dolly dressed as a glass of milk and an Oreo cookie — I'll let you work out which was which. One girl dressed as the Wicked Witch while her llama was dressed as Dorothy, complete with braided wig and blue checkered dress. One year Chip and Alice dressed as Mario and Luigi, from the Mario Brothers video game franchise — complete with go karts from the video game. There stood Chip, not only wearing the big red Mario cap on his head, but encased in a red cardboard go kart his girl Alice had put together for him. Though they may not understand the concept of winning, the llamas nonetheless agree to the hullabaloo that is the annual fair with very little complaint. In fact, most of them seem to love it.

Year after year, Chip proved his mistress's assessment as "the master of chill" during the costume competition. One year she dressed him as Napoleon Dynamite from the film of the same name, complete with giant, round-wire-frame glasses, curly blonde wig and t-shirt proclaiming: Vote For Pedro. He wore every costume without complaint—in fact, it seemed as though he understood the costumes made humans fawn over him, and he almost looked pleased with himself. I Tweeted out photos of Chip in his Napoleon Dynamite costume, standing calmly in the middle of a crowd of admirers, his girl Alice by his side, as if they were posing on the red carpet.

Year after year, we hyped up the llama coverage at the Douglas County Fair, until it came to the attention of the local NPR affiliate, who did a radio story on both the competition and the live Tweeting, which had gained a modest, but enthusiastic, following.

If anyone had told me when I started in the field of journalism 25 years ago that I'd end up being a llama correspondent, I probably would've wondered what drugs they were taking and where I could score some. But the truth of the matter is it's been a fulfilling, learning experience I wouldn't trade for anything.

*The names of all 4-H llama project kids and llamas have been changed to respect their privacy.

The Reason I Support Trans Folks

I first became aware of the trans community back in the early to mid 1990s when my best friend Michael came out as a gay man. Not that I didn't know trans people existed — I was aware a small portion of the population went through gender reassignment surgery (sex changes we called them back then), and honestly, I have always figured if someone was that serious about changing their gender, then that was their business, though I'd never met a trans person in real life. (That I knew of.)

Michael and I both love to dance, so I started going out to the gay clubs with him. I was married at the time, so going to gay clubs was a fun way to get to go dance without my husband worrying I was doing anything untoward.

My bestie Michael walked me through LGBTQ culture, explaining the customs and slang and such. One night we were hanging out in the club and my friend subtlety indicated toward a woman I thought was another gay man in drag, dressing fem — which is different than a drag queen, because drag is more performance art, but I digress.

I was one of just a handful of cis-women in the club, though "cis" wasn't a term we were using at that time.

"See her?" he said. "She had a sex change. She's a full woman now. Poor thing. Every time I see her, she's falling down drunk."

Michael and I understood without saying to each other that the trans woman wasn't always drunk because she had transitioned. Rather, she was always drunk because she had gone through with the transition and people — her own family? — still didn't want to accept her as a woman.

I glanced over at the woman who was slumped against the wall, barely able to stand, and our eyes locked. She smiled at me — a kind smile — and even though she was clearly impaired, her sad, knowing smile conveyed an entire idea — *All I want is to be accepted as you are accepted. Why is that so terrible?* In that instant, my heart broke. She was clearly in pain, all because people insist on being so small minded about things that really don't matter.

I smiled back at her. I tried to make my smile convey its own message — *I see you as a woman just as I am, and I accept you as you are* — but I don't know if she got that. Her smile still haunts me. Even though I can't really remember the details of her face, the memory of that smile remains. The thing is, she may very well be dead, either from substance abuse or violence, because the world is not kind to trans folks.

At the time, I'd had no trouble adjusting to the convention that drag queens were supposed to be referred to as "she" while in drag, but "he" while presenting as gay men, as my friend Michael taught me. It seemed perfectly logical.

In that one moment, I knew trans women were women and trans men were men. I knew it to my bones, just because. There is no reason to torture people over something that ultimately doesn't matter and destroy their lives in the process. Who knows what that woman could've accomplished if people had just let her live her life in peace?

It doesn't matter. Let it go.

The Penis to God is in Chicago

Recently, I had occasion to be in Chicago for the American Library Association Conference. I traveled there with a group of authors, and when we weren't at the conference, we of course had to take in the sights and tastes of Chicago, because it is a fabulous town.

One afternoon, an author friend and I took a shuttle to downtown and wandered for the day. I've been to Chicago a few times, but always only for a weekend, so I don't know it well.

After having lunch at Harry Carrey's, we walked the streets, marveling at the architecture, stepping into shops, and exploring the Chicago River Walk. Eventually, we wandered into a plaza in the middle of everything where we eavesdropped on a tour guide giving the histories of the various surrounding buildings.

But suddenly, one building caught my eye, but the tour guide's focus was in another direction. My curiosity was piqued.

I've seen European cathedrals — intricately artistic monuments to The

Chicago Temple Building

Almighty that undoubtedly took thousands of hours of thousands of lives to erect, but nothing like this. This appeared to be a church-skyscraper. A Sky-church-scraper? I'd never seen anything quite like it, and for some reason, I couldn't take my eyes off it. The weed we'd procured at a downtown dispensary that morning might've been part of the reason. I pointed it out to my friend.

"What is that? Is is a church? It's like a skyscraper..."

"With a cross on top," she finished. "That's a good question. Let's go check it out." So we walked over. Sure enough, it was church.

"Yep," she said, throwing her hands in the air. "It's a penis to God," and we both doubled over, laughing.

There were several gorgeous stained glass windows displayed on the ground level, telling the church's story.

The windows tell the story of how Chicago's first Methodists built a log cabin, which was replaced with a brick church until 1858, when church leaders dedicated a four-story, multi-use structure with stores and other businesses on the first two floors and church space for worship and classes on the top two floors.

That church-slash-commercial space burned down in the Great Chicago Fire of 1871. It was replaced with the current structure, the Chicago Temple building, which boasts 23 floors and was the tallest skyscraper in Chicago from 1924 to 1930, something the Methodists are quite proud of.

It seems to me this impressive, golden-tipped Midwestern phallus, rising triumphantly from the Great Plains, is not just a penis to God, but also a penis to capitalism. I also want to believe it's a big old middle finger to New York City and the Catholics, where

Chicago Temple Building Spire

St. Patrick's Cathedral in Midtown Manhattan stands a measly 329.6 feet to Chicago Temple's 568 feet.

And it makes sense the Methodists would choose Chicago for such an impressive monument. It was Methodist Circuit Riders who rode out on horseback to bring Christianity to the Great Plains and the West.

The Chicago Temple likes to bill itself the tallest church building in the world, but when you Google that phrase, various lists come up, and many of those lists don't include the Chicago Temple because the church doesn't use the whole building. While the church occupies the upper floors — including a sky chapel — the lower floors are mostly rented out to lawyers, because the church skyscraper is near the Cook County and US District Courts, a fact I find both appropriate and amusing.

Apparently we missed out by not going inside and riding the elevator all the way to the top to see the Sky Chapel, which is located underneath the spire, and decorated with beautiful stained glass windows, but I didn't find that out until I came home and researched the Chicago Temple Building.

The whole experience was fascinating, especially in light of current events and the melding of American evangelicalism with capitalism. Turns out it's nearly as old as America itself.

PART II

Letters from the Kansas Abortion Wars

Letters from the Kansas Abortion Wars

After Donald Trump was elected president in 2016, the direction of my life was forever changed. I began volunteering for the Kansas Abortion Fund, which at the time was still named the Peggy Bowman Second Chance Fund. (Peggy was a nurse for Doctor George Tiller, who performed later abortions in Wichita during the 1980s and Nineties and was gunned by an anti-abortion terrorist in his own church.)

In the years that followed my acceptance onto the Kansas Abortion Fund board, a whole series of nightmare scenarios played out: Ruth Bader Ginsberg died, President Pussygrabber stacked the Supreme Court with judges who had a clear forced-birth agenda, and suddenly, half the population didn't have basic protections over our own bodies, a right I had taken for granted since my birth in 1972, the same year Roe V. Wade was decided.

I assumed sitting on the board of an abortion fund would be mostly lowkey and uneventful, which it was — at first. Then in 2019, it all snowballed into an unfathomable, often frightening, sometimes wonderful, ride.

The following are a selection of my blog entries at Medium.com about joining the reproductive rights movement, learning the politics of abortion, and then scrambling to get Kansans out to vote to protect the rights of our daughters and trans sons.

I have the highest regard for the hardworking activists who have been willing to stand up for all our reproductive rights over the years. Being an activist with boots on the ground for reproductive rights means taking a public stand about a subject most people would rather avoid talking about altogether. I never thought I'd be an activist, but the attacks on women, trans people, Black and brown Americans and the entire LGBTQ+ community were too big to ignore, and I knew I could no longer sit quietly on the sidelines.

This is how I was radicalized.

April 15, 2019

The Reason I Joined the Board of an Abortion Fund

Because abortion is such a dirty word, I talk about it a lot less than I'd like, which would probably come as a surprise to some of my friends. See, a few years ago now, I joined the board of an abortion fund, so I talk about the importance of safe, legal abortion more than most people. Abortion is one of those things a lot of people don't like to think about, let alone talk about out loud. Many people have uncomfortable emotions surrounding the procedure, or believe they'll never need an abortion, or they figure past the age of needing one, so it's easier to just not think about abortion, and take for granted it will always be available.

But when trump was elected, I knew we were entering the Upside-Down. I realized for the first time in my life the country I call home might reverse some of women's long-fought-for rights. So I made the conscious decision to not only start thinking about abortion and abortion rights, but to take action.

Here's the thing: I didn't want to. I don't want to be this person. I don't want to have to fight for my rights, and my daughter's rights, and the rights of the bodily autonomy of every person in this country, but I also feel like I can't not fight for those things. To be clear, I am past the age of needing an abortion. This has nothing to do with my personal healthcare concerns. For me, this is an issue of rights and bodily autonomy, pure and simple.

So, to my friends and family out there wondering why I've gone full activist suddenly out of nowhere, this is why. I understand my newfound interest in abortion rights may be confusing, or even upsetting to you. I get it. I get that abortion makes people uncomfortable. All I can say is that I am more uncomfortable at the thought of the moms who will die in childbirth if we put the priority of her fetus' rights above hers. I am more dismayed at the thought of all the girls who will be forced to leave high school or college if they're denied the medical care they require. I am far more bothered by the thought of all the single mothers who will be forced even further into poverty, and this in a time when social services are being cut to the bone. I am more horrified by the fact that my country is currently violating the rights of immigrant girls by denying them the abortion care they have requested, effectively altering their bodies, their futures and their lives, forever. This thought is particularly horrifying when one considers the abuse and trauma they've already endured, and now, on top of everything else, we're going to force them to be mothers.

To me, that is unconscionable. My worry that this country may try to restrict constitutionally protected bodily autonomy has finally outweighed my apathy, and I have to say I haven't regretted a single second since I decided to get actively involved in the issue of abortion.

The thank you cards we receive from the patients our fund assists are like nothing I expected. I mean, I don't know exactly what I expected when I began volunteering for the fund, but so far, every single "thank you," we've received reveals the strength and hope of the person who sent it.

We've gotten letters from young single moms who are already working full time and simply can't afford another child. We get thank yous from married moms who need to be able to keep working or care for their special needs children. We receive thank yous from college girls who write to express their thanks because their education is too important to them to give up. We receive thank yous from people who have health issues that prevent them from carrying a child and going through childbirth. We receive thank yous from people who were carrying fetuses that weren't compatible with life. We receive thank yous from women in violent relationships they can't leave. We get thank yous from people addicted to drugs or alcohol who know they shouldn't be pregnant, let alone have a child. We get thank yous from those who don't identify as women.

We agree. We agree wholeheartedly with all of these people. They deserve choice. They deserve control over their lives and their futures, no matter how they ended up pregnant. We don't judge, and frankly, we don't care. We never ask for anything from the people we assist. They owe us nothing. They tell us their stories because they need to be able to unburden themselves to someone who won't judge them, and we don't. It's that simple.

Those thank yous are the reason I'm on the board of an abortion fund. Abortion care might be one of the most profound donations you can ever make, because no matter how small your donation, it is immediate and profound. Abortion fund volunteers don't make any money for what we do. Funds keep our expenses to a minimum to ensure the maximum amount of your donation goes directly to help the recipient.

But the fact remains that none of those stories are relevant. No one should be forced to share their intimate, personal pain to prove their humanity. People in need of abortion care have a constitutional right to access that care, without shame and without having to prove their need. Abortion is a necessary legal medical procedure. As such it is only the business of the person accessing abortion care.

And for those who would put the "personhood" of a fetus above the undeniable personhood of the actual people who send us those handwritten thank yous, I will never be able to agree with your point of view. It's easy to vote for an antichoice candidate. It's easy to claim to be on the side of "babies." What's not easy is to hear real people's fear because they're pregnant and they don't have insurance. Or that someone's developmentally delayed daughter was raped and now needs an abortion. It's not a good feeling to know so many millions of Americans are working for such low pay they often simply can't afford an additional child in their family.

As an individual citizen, I don't have any power over decisions the Supreme Court may make in regard to abortion and personal autonomy. Though I always make sure to vote, in local, regional and national elections, my vote is only one vote. Volunteering for, and donating to, my state's abortion fund has given me a way to take an active role in making sure everyone in my state is able to access the abortion care they need.

October 23, 2019

Abortion Funds to the Rescue

I was in my forties when I first learned about abortion funds. I remember marveling at the dedication it must take to work at raising money for such a controversial medical procedure—and then

I kind of forgot about abortion funds—Until the 2018 presidential election. I was so furious to see a man, so obviously unfit for the job of president, chosen over a woman who was more than qualified I could barely function. I was so angry I knew that if I didn't channel that energy constructively, it'd poison me from the inside out.

What's the most feminist thing I could possibly do? I wondered. What's the most libtard, anti-misogynist action I take, that's also positive, so I can burn off some of this fury?

The answer hit me like a thunderbolt: Abortion. I could become an activist in reproductive rights. It was perfect. I felt like Wonder Woman discovering my powers and leaving Paradise Island. I contacted our state's abortion fund—the Peggy Bowman Second Chance Fund of Kansas—and offered to help in whatever way I could. The women quickly embraced me and invited me to serve on the board.

It's the most satisfying volunteer work I've ever participated in, and I've learned so much:

Abortion funds are all over the country. Many serve their state, but some serve a large city, like Chicago (Chicago Abortion Fund or CAF), Washington D.C. (DC Abortion Fund or DCAF) and New York City (Abortion Fund for Planned Parenthood of NYC).

Abortion funds very much want to help anyone who is low on cash and needing abortion care. Our goal is remove the barrier of cost to anyone who needs an abortion.

Most, but not all, abortion funds belong to the National Network of Abortion Funds (NNAF). NNAF helps all of its member funds tap into the entire nation to raise funds, through events like the Bowl-A-Thon, which abortion funds all over the country take part in every April.

Every abortion fund volunteer I've ever met works for their fund for free. I'm not saying abortion funds don't have to occasionally hire help, but I haven't met a paid person yet.

Every abortion fund volunteer I've met is deeply dedicated to the idea of bodily autonomy and equal rights for everyone.

Because every abortion fund is a little different, we offer different levels of help and/or services. In addition to providing cash to help with the cost of an abortion, some abortion funds offer services like rides to the clinic and childcare, or extra monetary help for costs like hotel rooms.

We WANT you to access our help. We're all working to be more mindful and inclusive, so that no one feels shame or judgment when accessing our funds.

Even if you don't ever directly speak to anyone from the fund, you should the people who volunteer for abortion funds really do care about you and your right to live your life as you see fit. If an abortion is part of your life plan, then we support you in that decision.

This month, the fund I volunteer for, the Peggy Bowman Second Chance Fund, changed our name to the Kansas Abortion Fund. It was not a decision made in haste. It was a discussion we had for more than a year. The Peggy Bowman Second Chance Fund was named for Peggy Bowman, an iconic feminist and reproductive rights activist in Wichita. Peggy was the executive director for Planned Parenthood Wichita and later, the lobbyist for Dr. George Tiller, one of the country's few doctors who performed later abortions. After right-wing blowhard Bill O'Reilly spent weeks spewing dangerous rhetoric on the Fox News Channel about Dr. Tiller, Dr. Tiller was gunned down by an antichoice terrorist in his own church, on Sunday morning, in front of the congregation. Peggy remained active in the community until her natural death in 2016.

In Peggy Bowman's memory, the Kansas Abortion Fund has created the Peggy Bowman Fund, a supplemental fund we maintain to assist Kansans who need more specialized (expensive) abortion care, or who need to travel out of state.

These are frightening times in America, and in the face of increasing legislation to restrict women's healthcare, we decided incorporating the word "Abortion" into our name was critical. The time is right. We're done apologizing for the word "Abortion," and we won't be shamed into staying silent.

Author's note: I didn't write about abortion much in 2020, but by 2021 it was no secret in the reproductive rights movement that Roe would be overturned, it was just a question of when. The public didn't seem to understand the threat until Texas banned all abortion after six weeks, even in cases of incest and rape, on September 1, 2021. That's when people began to realize conservatives would take their plan nationwide, as several other states announced their intention to do enact copycat laws, especially if Roe were to be overturned.

The shift in public opinion was palpable. Spontaneous reproductive rights marches popped up and they wanted the Kansas Abortion Fund to participate. Up until this point, we'd gone basically unseen, with a modest social media following, and getting people to donate was getting to be like pulling teeth, especially with so many folks feeling the squeeze of inflation.

Suddenly, the Kansas Abortion Fund was being invited to host our table at events and our president began to be inundated with requests to speak at functions, not to mention field interviews from journalists. When Roe fell, it was almost like people associated with abortion funds went from being social pariahs to rock stars. It became difficult for the Kansas Abortion Fund to attend every event and get back to every journalist. At one point three board members were fielding interviews from journalists all over the world (thank goodness I wasn't one of them), and we all had to divvy up the duties of appearing at events, answering emails, fielding phone calls and gracefully accepting huge donations from the most unexpected sources. Comedian and actress Sarah Silverman meant to send a large check to our national umbrella organization, the National Network of Abortion Funds, but somehow the check landed in the Kansas Abortion Fund's PO Box. Our president contacted NNAF, who reached out to Sarah, who graciously let the Kansas Abortion Fund keep a sizeable chunk of that check, while the rest went to NNAF as originally intended. The band Paramore committed to donating $1 of their ticket sales to KAF when they played Sandstone in October of 2022, and they let us set up a table there, where we sold an incredible number of abortion-positive t-shirts and hoodies. The number of small donations we received from individuals increased by something like a bajillion percent, and people donated from all over the country and the world.

It was perhaps the first time ever we didn't have to beg people for money. Instead, they were throwing it at us. But we knew at some point it would all come to an end, and we'd slide back into obscurity, begging for donations. That's why the Kansas Abortion Fund is still operating as frugally as we did before all the attention and money. What's changed is we've been able to increase the amount we give to Kansans in need of abortion care, as well as expand funding to patients who are above the poverty line but still at financial risk. We've also increased the amount we give to patients who are forced to get later abortions, as those procedures are often more expensive than giving birth to a baby in a hospital.

October 25, 2021

People Are Angry About the new Texas Abortion Law

I make so secret of the fact I'm on the board of the Kansas Abortion Fund. If you don't know what abortion funds are, we raise donations from the public so that people in our states in need of abortion care, but short on cash, are not blocked from getting the care they need. Abortion is a time-sensitive treatment, and since many states block federal funds, state funds, and even private insurance from paying for abortions, private citizens have opted to help out those folks who can't be pregnant, for whatever reason. Abortion funds don't judge. We don't care why you need the abortion, we just want you to be able to access the care.

Last weekend, the Kansas Abortion Fund was asked to attend several Women's Marches across the state. We were able to have tables in Topeka, Kansas City and Lawrence, but you may be surprised to learn Kansas also had Women's Marches on Oct. 2 in Manhattan, Hays, Salina and Pittsburg. (For those of you who aren't familiar, those cities are deep in political red country.)

I was privileged enough to attend the Women's March in Lawrence, and this rally felt different than other ones I've been to in the last five years.

People were vocally angry, dismayed, and exhausted that conservatives are coming for their rights in this way. They gravitated to our table out of clear, visible desperation for something concrete they could do, because they could not believe things had gotten this far out of hand concerning abortion rights. Three different women older than me revealed it was their very first protest ever. We're talking about women who were alive for the Civil Rights movement in the Sixties and the Women's movements of the 1970s and didn't protest. Last Saturday, though, they came out.

"I have six granddaughters and I can't believe I'm having to fight for their right to an abortion," one woman told me. She also revealed she'd talked with two of them about abortion for the very first time, and she'd been hesitant because she didn't know what their opinions on abortion were and she wasn't sure if they'd be offended or angry with her. Then she smiled because it all worked out okay. As it turned out, her granddaughters were also both pro-choice, and they appreciated their grandmother talking about her beliefs openly. She thinks it helped their relationship.

"I think it's important to talk with them," she told me. "They need to understand what their rights are."

One first-time protestor spoke with me about how she grew up in San Francisco with her two moms in the 1970s, but then the family moved to Michigan, and there, she couldn't tell anyone she had two moms. "They even had to go so far as to sleep in different bedrooms so people wouldn't find out," she said, wistfully. "Things are better now but…"

"We still have a long way to go," I finished for her. We both understood that even though she was talking about LGBTQIA+ rights, abortion rights are connected, because all discriminatory laws have one thing in common: limiting the power of certain groups, including LGBTQIA folks, Americans of color in general and women of all races.

"That's right," she replied, nodding. She pulled her jacket open to show me her protest t-shirt she'd made that morning with a Sharpie. **Abortion AF**, it proclaimed.

I saw families there with their little girls, openly talking to them about abortion and their constitutional right to abortion care. They'd bring the girls right up to our table and we encouraged people to take a button or a sticker. I saw moms pin "Abortion is Health Care" buttons on their young girls. People donated and grabbed t-shirts that said Kansas Abortion Fund or Ad Abortion Per Aspera (our state motto is Ad Aspera Per Aspera, which is Latin for "to the stars through difficulties.")

I've never seen a response like it. People were hungry for information and what they could do to stop the attacks on women and trans men's bodies. There was a palpable feeling of urgency. Normally, when we have our abortion fund table up, people are shy.

They often glance at us nervously and walk away. Most folks are hesitant to wear a button that says "abortion," let alone a t-shirt, and many won't even say the word.

There was none of that last weekend. No one was mincing words, and no one was hiding behind euphemisms or polite language. Suddenly, people realized "Pro-choice" had become too benign, so they were openly saying the word "abortion," in talking about their rights. No one seemed at all shy about having the word abortion on t-shirts and protest signs. We gave out all our t-shirts and most of our buttons and stickers.

There was also a collective feeling of unity, and everyone at the protest seemed eager to be inclusive and intersectional, even if these were new concepts to them.

We made sure to tell folks about the upcoming vote in Kansas that will copycat the Texas law if pro-choice folks don't get out to vote. Of course, the conservative Kansas Legislature has made sure to put this vote on a primary ballot in August of 2022, because historically, primary elections have the lowest turnout.

What happened in Texas can happen anywhere, and that's exactly what radical right wingers are aiming for. There are now copycat laws being proposed in Arkansas, Florida, South Dakota, Idaho, Indiana, Oklahoma, Missouri, South Carolina, Ohio, and my home state of Kansas.

This time, though, I think conservatives have overplayed their hand and it's going to bite them on the ass, hard. They don't seem to understand the fury they've awoken. People are angry.

December 10, 2021

Many Men Don't Seem to Understand How Much Time, Money & Worry Women Spend on Not Getting Pregnant

During my years on this earth, I have found many men don't seem to want to think about birth control whatsoever, which I get. Who wants to think about a boner-killer like pregnancy when all you want is to get laid?

Must be nice.

Women don't have that luxury. Ever. Instead, we have kindly acquiesced in taking care of most of the pregnancy worries and not bothering men with the details. The problem with that is many men don't seem to understand what all women go through to not get pregnant.

"You can't spend a few dollars at the drug store on birth control?" A man asked me once, because he seemed to think anyone just walk into a drug store and access all sorts of birth control methods. Nope. The only over the counter birth control one can purchase at a drug store are spermicides and condoms, and of course condoms require male cooperation. But men don't like condoms, and some will even go so far as to go through the theatrics of putting one on only to slip it off just before insertion.

Better methods of birth control, like the pill, require yearly doctor's visits — that's time off work and at a minimum a copay — and the pills themselves can cost anywhere between $20 and $50 per month. I can hear people out there now thinking to themselves — "I thought birth control was free thanks to Obamacare."

That was the promise, but of course the insurance companies have found all sorts of legal loopholes out of that promise — like only offering certain brands for free — and trump provided them even more loopholes in the name of "religious freedom." Now insurance companies can pretty much refuse to cover any birth control method for any reason. If they happen to cover the brand you prefer, that's great. If they suddenly decide they're not going to, they can do that, at any time. Since the implementation of the Affordable Care Act, the cost of my birth control pills have fluctuated in price from $0 per month to $10 per month to $20 per month to $50 per month, all for the exact same prescription.

"What does the brand of birth control have to do with anything?" I can hear men asking. Well, they're made with differing levels of estrogen and progestin, and each formulation can affect various women very differently. The side effects of birth control pills are plentiful and unpleasant and include (ironically) lower sex drive, weight gain, depression, nausea, between-period spotting and headaches. Finding the right birth control pill can take a lot of time and money to figure out which one causes the least number of side effects. I myself went though five different brands before finding one that didn't make me so depressed I wanted to shoot myself in the face. This took literally years, because one must give each brand a few months to see how it's ultimately going to work before switching to another. Once I finally settled on one pill that wasn't too horrible, the weight gain and moodiness my husband and I just had to live with.

Then there are men like Rush Limbaugh who don't understand how birth control pills work at all. Rush thought women could just pop a pill when they plan to have sex. He, and many other men, don't seem to understand the pill must be taken daily — and preferably about the same time of day each day — or they can fail. Even if a woman isn't having sex, she has to continue to take those pills every single day or risk pregnancy when she finally does decide to have sex.

Other birth control methods that require expensive doctor's visits include IUDs, hormone implants, hormone shots, hormone patches and vaginal rings. These methods, which are generally more effective than birth control pills, can cost somewhere between $200 and $2,000 without insurance — and even a few hundred dollars with insurance — because again, insurance companies can opt to not pay to cover 100% of the cost of certain brands of birth control devices.

Here's the kicker: Even when we're on a prescribed method of birth control administered by a doctor, women still worry about getting pregnant because it happens all the time.

"Just have the baby," men often say, without a care in the world.

Sigh.

Even with insurance, the out-of-pocket expense of having a baby in a hospital in the US is somewhere in the neighborhood of $3,000 to $5,000. If your baby has to spend time in the NICU, that price can rise to $10,000. That's with insurance. Those millions of Americans who are having babies without insurance? They're often sentenced to a life of poverty due to unpaid medical bills, and some towns are now arresting people for the offence, even though it's supposed to be unconstitutional in the US to incarcerate people for being poor.

Some men seem to think that because pregnancy and childbirth are "natural," that means they are risk-free. Nothing could be further from the truth. The overall death rate for pregnant women in the US is now 33 deaths per 100,000 live births, one of the worst death rates in so-called "first world" countries. If you're a Black woman, that rate jumps to 70 deaths per 100,000 live births.

But even a successful pregnancy and childbirth experience can cause permanent injuries to women, including nerve damage, incontinence (bladder and/or bowel), and lifelong, debilitating pain. In addition, many women are forced to take time off work during and after pregnancy to care for their own health and then, of course, to care for the baby once born. That salary loss can be devastating.

So for any man out there wondering why women become so angry about childbearing and abortion issues, the answer is simply this: We are stressed out, and we've been largely left to our own devices to figure out paying for the costs of birth control, child care, child birth and pregnancy. Even a man who has his wages garnished for an unwanted pregnancy won't pay a fraction of the amount the woman is forced to pay. Now, with Roe V Wade likely to be axed, millions of women will have to travel hundreds, even thousands of miles for abortion care, because apparently this country believes women haven't been inconvenienced or punished enough for sex.

February 26, 2022

Let's Be Clear: Texas Didn't Outlaw Abortion, They Outsourced It

Now that Texas's new unconstitutional abortion law has been in effect for a few months, we know a few things — Texans needing abortion care haven't stopped getting abortions. They're just leaving Texas and traveling to Oklahoma, Missouri, Arkansas and Kansas. Know how I know? Because I volunteer for the Kansas Abortion Fund and the clinics here are telling us they're absolutely overrun — and I mean overrun — with Texas patients. The funds and clinics in Oklahoma, Missouri and Arkansas are reporting the same, and the data bears this out. Abortion care providers in Kansas saw a 9% increase in patients in 2020 compared with 2019, and 52% of their patients were from out-of-state[1].

Something else we know is every time "prolifers" pass another law discouraging abortion, the statistics for later abortions go up. Imagine that. When people have simple access to a safe, legal procedure, they terminate earlier. When people are forced to take off work to endure waiting periods and travel out of state, it takes them longer to get together the funds for their procedures, which pushes their abortions later and later. This is a curious outcome of their laws, because most "prolifers" would say they're particularly against later terminations. After all, that's ostensibly why they limited abortions to six weeks in Texas — to stop later abortions. The problem is, many women don't know they're pregnant at six weeks, and the majority are still going to get the abortion. Because of the types of laws "prolifers" like to pass, many people end up not being able to terminate until they're 18, 19, 20 weeks along. Some people end up forced to terminate early in the second term at 22 or 24 weeks. Most of those people would have had their abortion far earlier with simpler access.

Ultimately, what's probably going to happen is Roe Vs. Wade will be overturned and abortion will become a "state's rights" issue. (Which, by the way, is horse shit, because my federal constitutional rights should not change from state to state, and bodily autonomy is a basic constitutional right.) With abortion only being legal in certain states, rest assured we will continue to see abortions skewing to later terminations, especially when some people will be forced to travel several states away, or to Canada or Mexico where people with uteruses are apparently viewed as — people.

My state, Kansas, is set to try to pass a copycat law of the Texas one this August during our primaries. (Because of course, far fewer people come out to vote in primary elections, and people who are pro-choice are far less likely to vote.) There are politicians in several other states planning on passing so-called Texas copycat abortion laws, including Missouri, Arkansas, Oklahoma, Florida, South Dakota, Idaho[2] and probably others. That means Texans needing abortion care will have to travel even farther than they are now, and easy access will disappear for millions more Americans, which will absolutely cause many people to terminate later than they want to.

Thankfully, there is now medication abortion, which can be administered very early and is medically indistinguishable from miscarriage, as both involve identical hormones. However, US conservatives are already passing laws to make receiving abortion drugs in the mail illegal in their states.[3] Conservatives are also passing laws to prevent doctors prescribing the drugs over video calls with patients, insisting patients must be seen in person. That might sound reasonable, except that out here in flyover country, some people are literally hundreds of miles away from the nearest doctor, they're used to having telemedicine visits already, and abortion medication is incredibly safe[4]. However, medication abortion is only effective up to about 10 weeks of pregnancy, and if people are forced to travel out of state to pick up their medication, putting them past the 10-week mark, they may end up having to schedule a surgical abortion instead.

Welcome to the United States of Divided Rights, where one political group has managed to concretely ensure a very real outcome that's in direct conflict with one of their stated goals — to end later abortions.

1. Associated Press; "Abortions in Kansas see largest annual increase since 1995"; June 1, 2021, https://www.kmbc.com/article/abortions-in-kansas-increased-by-91-in-2020-kansas-department-of-health-and-environment/36600344
2. Openheim, Oren; "Which states' lawmakers have said they might copy Texas' abortion law"; September 23, 2021, https://abcnews.go.com/Politics/states-lawmakers-copy-texas-abortion-law/story?id=79818701
3. Sullivan, Kaitlyn; "At-home abortion medication requests soared after Texas restrictions"; NBC News; February 25, 2022, https://www.nbcnews.com/health/health-news/-home-abortion-medication-requests-soared-texas-restrictions-rcna17634
4. Guttmacher Institute; February 1, 2021, https://www.guttmacher.org/evidence-you-can-use/medication-abortion

May 8, 2022

Abortions for Rape, Incest and Fetal Deformities are NOT Rare

The primary argument we're hearing from conservatives right now in defense of their disgusting, unconstitutional push to overturn Roe V Wade is that the vast majority of abortions are performed for "convenience," and not for crimes like rape and incest, or because of health concerns like a danger to the pregnant person or fetal anomalies, some fatal.

Let's dig into some numbers: In 2017, approximately 862,320 abortions were performed in the US. The rate of girls aged 14 and under who were treated to remove a pregnancy for that year was 0.2

percent. That means that in 2017, 1,724 girls aged 14 or younger in the United States of America received abortion treatment. Not the year 1950, but in 2017.

Does that sound rare to you? Or does that sound like a fucking nightmare? Now just imagine if half the states ban abortion. How many hundreds of little girls might be forced to go through the trauma of pregnancy and childbirth?

What's even more troubling is a significant percentage of teenage girls who become pregnant are impregnated by a grown-ass man. Thing is, we don't really know the numbers very well, because no one keeps track of that. The only concrete data we have comes from a study done by the Guttmacher institute on data collected in 1988, while the study itself was released in 1997. It showed that "among mothers aged 15–17 who had a child in 1988, 27% had a partner at least five years older than themselves." (Why was the data for girls aged 14 and under left out of this study? Who knows.) The same study showed 39% of 15-year-old girls were impregnated by a man aged 20 to 29.

Data consistently shows that ectopic pregnancies, in which the embryo implants itself somewhere outside the uterus (often in a fallopian tube) occurs in about 1.97% of US pregnancies, meaning that out of every 1,000 pregnancies, 19 or 20 are ectopic. Ectopic pregnancies that don't self-abort (miscarry) must be treated by a doctor, or the pregnant person has a huge chance of dying by bleeding out if the pregnancy ruptures the fallopian tube. According to the CDC, in 2020 the US saw 3,605,201 births, meaning about 6,000 to 7,000 American women and trans men had to have an ectopic pregnancy terminated. Even rabid right-to-lifer Lila Rose admits these pregnancies must be terminated, but plenty of conservative politicians think ectopic pregnancies can be removed from a fallopian tube and "re-implanted" in the uterus, which is complete fantasy. The procedure doesn't exist because it's impossible.

I don't even know how to address the pregnancies that occur from the rape of adult women. The official statistic in this country is that one in five women are raped, but most American women will attest that's a laughably low number. Rape is vastly underreported and almost never successfully prosecuted in this country — only six out of every thousand rapists will go to prison.

Though conservatives would have us believe that it's legal to have an abortion right up to birth and even beyond, that of course is nonsense — the fact is fewer than 1% of abortions in this country happen at 21 weeks or later. (A "normal" human pregnancy lasts 40 weeks.) I couldn't find a breakdown of the percentage of those later abortions that are performed for fetal anomalies, versus a danger to the health of the mother, versus the patients who were forced to abort later because of access barriers. But loosely based on 2017's numbers, one percent of 826,000+ abortions means at least a few thousand were performed to either save the pregnant person's life or because the fetus had significant anomalies. Again, does that sound like a small number? At a minimum, that's several thousand pregnancies every single year that average American families have to agonize over.

Additionally, the fact so many conservatives (usually conservative men) characterize pregnancy and childbirth as "inconvenient," and frame the choice to either give up a child or raise a child as an "inconvenience," is infuriating. It is "inconvenient" when I can't get a reservation at my favorite restaurant. Raising a child isn't just "inconvenient." It is literally the most important, impactful decision any human being can make. To treat raising a child as if it's equal to purchasing a puppy from the pet store shows an abysmal disrespect for human life that frankly, makes me ill.

The right might as well come right out and say it: *Women do not matter. Children do not matter. The use and abuse of women and children is something we heartily support.*

If conservatives want fewer abortions, there are proven ways of achieving just that. My favorite example is Colorado, where an incredibly successful free IUD program has halved the number of abortions in the state, while also decreasing welfare payments by millions of dollars. Incredibly, conservatives in Colorado tried to stop the program, but the public wouldn't let them.

The horrifying human rights violation US conservatives are trying to pull off is an absolute travesty.

May 24, 2022

Supreme Court Justice Alito is Wrong

It's incredibly frustrating the way the radical religious right leans on pure lies in their opposition to abortion, and the rot goes all the way to the top, from the Pope to leaders of nations and even Supreme Court Justices. Of course, the country has been in an uproar over Samuel Justice Alito's leaked opinion on abortion, in which he so boldly claimed:

"The inescapable conclusion is that a right to abortion is not deeply rooted in the Nation's history and traditions." -Justice Samuel Alito, forced-birth shill

The problem with that statement is it's one-hundred-percent horseshit. Thankfully, NPR and other news outlets have begun reporting the truth. Not only does the United States of America have a long history of abortion, Founding Father Ben Franklin himself published a book that gave folks instructions for inducing their own abortions at home. (It was a general knowledge manual a family might own, with recipes, livestock tips, and some home medical remedies, including a list of herbal abortifacients.)

Every society has a history of abortion.[1] All of them. Abortion is ubiquitous, all over the planet.

There's evidence to suggest that during periods of witch burnings in Europe and America, many of the women (and a few men) who were condemned as witches were actually healers and midwives who were burned alive at the stake or tortured to death.[2]

So it's horrifying that Judge Alito cited a 17th century British judge named Sir Matthew Hale[3] as precedent for repealing Roe V Wade. Hale had two elderly women— Amy Duny and Rose Cullender— sentenced to hang, March 10, 1662, for the crime of witchcraft during the Bury St. Edmunds witch trials.[4] Hale also wrote a treatise stating marital rape couldn't exist because a wife's body belonged to her husband. That treatise influenced the laws on marital rape in the United States as late as 1993, when it officially became a crime in all fifty states. (Damn libruhls.)

All this time we've been gaslighted into believing we're being "hysterical" over abortion rights, when one of our very own Supreme Court Justices is revealed to be a ghoul whose hero is a woman-hating Puritan from the mid-1600s. Hale's witch trial took place just thirty years prior to the Salem Witch Trials.

Can this shit get any weirder?

Before doctors and hospitals, people went to their local healer or midwife for all kinds of ailments, assistance with births, and yes, tonics and teas that induced abortion. In times of famine, or if a family was simply overwhelmed with children already, aborting early on — before "quickening" — was common practice. At the same time in history when women were pushed out of the business of midwifery in favor of giving birth in modern hospitals overseen by male doctors, abortion began to be policed and criminalized.

Abortion isn't new. What is new — very new — is the idea abortion should be abolished. This didn't come about until the 1970s when conservative, evangelical politicians and their supporting clergy started pushing abortion as a pure outrage issue to gain voters. Their arguments — almost all of which are pure lies — have now reached a fevered pitch of madness. Today's forced birthers go so far as to claim it's legal to murder healthy babies in the United States, even after they've been born. Why anyone would choose to believe such a grizzly lie about their own country is beyond comprehension.

1. Serrano, Beatriz; "Why abortion is deeply rooted in the history of humankind"; El País; May 13, 2022, https://english.elpais.com/society/2022-05-13/abortion-is-deeply-rooted-in-the-history-of-humankind.html
2. Climo, Lillian, "A Note from the Collections: Midwives and Healers in the European Witch Trials," International Museum of Surgical Science, December 18, 2019, https://imss.org/2019/12/18/a-note-from-the-collections-midwives-and-healers-in-the-european-witch-trials/
3. Taub, Amanda, "The 17th-Century Judge at the Heart of Today's Women's Rights Rulings," New York Times, May 19, 2022, https://www.nytimes.com/2022/05/19/world/asia/abortion-lord-matthew-hale.html
4. https://www.visit-burystedmunds.co.uk/blog/bury-st-edmunds-witch-trials

June 25, 2022

No, You Being Asked to Mask & Vaccinate is Not "The Same" As Forced Pregnancy & Childbirth

In the wake of the illegitimate Supreme Court taking away bodily autonomy from people with uteruses, I'm seeing a lot of conservatives smugly state something to the effect that liberals had no qualms about bodily autonomy when it came to masks and vaccines.

I've seen a few conservative women make this statement, but usually, it's men. White men. White men who are still throwing a temper tantrum because they were politely asked to do something unselfish to benefit their country during a global pandemic. They seem to think the Supreme Court forcing people to carry and birth pregnancies they can't afford or don't want is an equal level of personal violation as having to wear a face mask in public, or get a flu shot — a flu shot — to keep their jobs.

Do you know why they think that? Because they are soft, spoiled, selfish baby-men, that's why.

Many of us out there have been pregnant, birthed babies, and raised those babies. We've also gotten flu shots. If one more man says out loud that these two things are "the same" women should have the right to blast them in the crotch with a flamethrower.

When did conservative men get so whiny and weak? Aren't these the guys who always say they're willing to put their bodies on the line for their country? That they're willing to bleed for the flag? But they can't get a flu shot? Are you fucking kidding me, fellas? Do you really think you could handle forty weeks of pregnancy, then labor, which lasts hours or days, then birth ripping open your nether regions when you can't handle a fucking *flu shot*?

And to top it all off, I they decided it was "liberals" who "made them" mask and vaccinate, so, therefore, I guess, the conservative "logic" goes, liberal women, whores had to have their bodily autonomy taken away, too! Because stomp, stomp, cry, cry! Conservative men, meanwhile, have no fucking clue they're punishing all the women in their own lives as well, because conservative women abort pregnancies just as often as liberal women do.[1] But of course, conservative women refuse to ever speak out or stand up for legal abortion, so it was always up to liberal women to uphold their rights for them, while they crossed their fingers and voted for tax cuts and white supremacy. (Except, of course, for all the ultra-rich Republicans who have no qualms about flying a woman wherever she needs to go to obtain her abortion.)

Truthfully, conservatives know pregnancy and childbirth are far bigger burdens than masks and vaccines. They just don't give a shit.

Conservatives believe the USA is for them and them only. Whatever it takes for them to have an advantage in society is fair game. When they say they're "originalists," they mean it. They want to go back to a constitution that only guaranteed rights for wealthy and maybe middle-class white men. Everyone else can go kick rocks and eat dirt as far as they care.

Hilariously, their even more gutless leader trump is reportedly quite worried the overturning of Roe might be the end of his political career:

"He keeps shitting all over his greatest accomplishment. When you speak to him, it's the response of someone fearing the backlash and fearing the politics of what happens when conservatives actually get what they want [on abortion]," says one source.[2]

And that really begs the question: Now that they've gone ahead and blown their collective wad all over the rest of us, and pulled their biggest bullshit stunt, what do conservatives have left to offer their constituents? The repeal of gay marriage? The banning of contraceptives? Do they really think they can keep winning on hate and whining? Because they have not achieved the flex they thought they would.

1. Dastagir, Alia, "When it comes to abortion, conservative women aren't a monolith," USA Today, May 28, 2019, https://www.usatoday.com/story/news/nation/2019/05/22/abortion-law-republican-and-conservative-women-dont-all-agree/3749202002/
2. Ramirez, Nikki McCann and Suebsaeng, Asawin, "In Private, Trump 'Keeps Shitting All Over' the End of Roe v. Wade, June 24, 2022, https://www.rollingstone.com/politics/politics-news/trump-roe-dobbs-abortion-midterms-1374049/

August 3, 2022

FOREVER THE FREE STATE: KANSAS VOTES NO

Yesterday, Kansans turned out in numbers rivaling a presidential election to resoundingly vote down amending the Kansas Constitution so that forced-birth extremists could completely ban abortion. The forced birthers brought this vote to the people because a few years ago, the Kansas Supreme Court declared abortion an inherent right in our constitution, so their only option was to try for amendment — not during a general election, mind you, but during a primary, hoping for low voter turnout.

Throughout their campaign, the forced birthers lied, and lied and LIED. They named their ridiculous measure "Value them Both," which was infuriating to Kansas women, and the wording of the measure was deliberately misleading, not to mention complete word salad. Look at this ridiculousness:

Regulation of abortion.

Because Kansans value both women and children, the constitution of the state of Kansas does not require government funding of abortion and does not create or secure a right to abortion. To the extent permitted by the constitution of the United States, the people, through their elected state representatives and state senators, may pass laws regarding abortion, including, but not limited to, laws that account for cirumstances of pregnancy resulting from rape or incest, or circumstances of necessity to save the life of the mother

○ Yes
○ No

The forced birthers kept insisting this vote wouldn't ban abortion—which was technically true—but their ultimate goal was a complete ban, which was confirmed when one of the "Value them Both" people was recorded stating as much.[1]

Perhaps realizing the vote might not go their way, the forced birthers went so far as to send out a mass text to Kansans a few days before the vote, stating that voting "yes" would preserve women's rights:

We soon learned the text was funded by Former US Rep. Tim Huelselkamp who represented Kansas in Congress from 2011–2017, and the text was totally legal according to Kansas election law.[2]

Which illustrates the dichotomy of Kansas. Though we're a "red" state, we're a stubborn, independent people who don't like to be told what to do, and we voted NO 60% to 40% in favor of allowing women and girls to keep control of their own bodies.

To be honest, most Kansans — even us progressive ones — were expecting the worst, or at least we expected the vote to be closer. I was hoping for a NO blowout, but the YES campaign was heavily funded by the Catholic Church, while the NO side was funded almost solely by individuals donating their hearts out.

Perhaps most importantly, the results of the midterm vote in Kansas shocked national pundits and activists, and has given real hope to Democrats and progressives across the country that we can take back our nation and save it from fascism.

Kansas' motto is Ad Aspera Per Aspera — to the stars through difficulties — and the Kansas Abortion Fund's motto is Ad Abortion Per Aspera for good reason.

1. Alcock, Andy, "Audio recording sheds light on potential legislation if Kansas 'Value Them Both' amendment passes," KMBC News, July 18, 2022 https://www.kmbc.com/article/recording-sheds-light-on-kansas-legislation-if-value-them-both-amendment-passes/40645319#
2. Smith, Sherman, "Former U.S. Rep. Tim Huelskamp connected to false text about Kansas abortion amendment," Kansas Reflector, August 2, 2022

August 9, 2022

Why Is the Forced-Birth Movement So Unnecessarily Cruel?

For years, progressives in the US have been fighting for affordable healthcare, and safety nets for the poor. And for years, conservatives have fought those measures tooth and nail, citing "freedom" and "fiscal responsibility."

Of course, there's one freedom conservatives can't abide and that's abortion — because, they claim, they "love babies." But being pregnant and having a baby is incredibly expensive, and often women's earning potential falls after she's had a child. In fact, the number one reason people cite for having an abortion is economic.[1] Poor women in the US often have trouble even coming up with the $600-$1,000 to end their first-trimester pregnancy, let alone pay for the birth and care of a baby.

But now that conservatives have succeeded in trashing Roe V Wade, they still won't even discuss issues such as raising the minimum wage, or paid maternity leave, or free, accessible birth control. So far, the only "solutions" conservatives offer for the people they've denied abortion are so-called Crisis Pregnancy Centers and Baby Drop Boxes.

Conservatives are eager to point to Crisis Pregnancy Centers as proof of their sincerity in wanting to assist poor women, and many are proud to say they donate. CPCs are proliferating across the US, with CPCs now outnumbering abortion clinics 3 to 1. The problem is CPCs offer very little actual help to pregnant women and new moms. In fact, the assistance is usually so little as to be laughable, and some red states are now redirecting tax dollars to CPCs, while continuing to cut social safety nets.

Crisis Pregnancy centers offer sonograms, but not for medical reasons, because CPCs are not medical facilities. They only use sonograms to try to guilt people into keeping their pregnancies. CPCs can't offer medical check-ups to the mother during the pregnancy, and pregnancies require several expensive doctor's appointments. CPCs don't help with paying for housing or childcare so that new moms can work. They don't offer help with utility bills or hospital bills.

In general, CPCs might give away some baby clothes, formula, prenatal vitamins and diapers to pregnant and new moms, but little else. Many CPCs don't even offer necessities like car seats or cribs, and those that do have strings attached. One CPC in Texas requires potential moms and/or dads to take parenting classes so they can "earn" points to choose baby equipment:

Our priority at the pregnancy center is the abortion determined woman. ...The promise of new baby items makes a difference to a woman in a crisis pregnancy situation. When a young lady walks into the grace closet, and witness God's provision, her imagined "boogie man" disappears. The fear of lack, or fear of "I will not be able to provide", or "I cannot have this baby because I cannot give my baby what it deserves" no longer exists. [2]

Did you catch that? This crisis pregnancy center admits in writing they have no interest in helping poor pregnant women who want to keep their babies. They're only interested in changing the minds of women who want to abort by dangling new baby items in front them. The reason for this, in their words, is they "don't want to duplicate services already available in the community" — services they routinely vote against.

Even worse, many CPCs will flat-out lie to pregnant women[3] to get them to keep their pregnancies. They tell women abortion might leave them sterile (highly unlikely), or that abortion causes long-term psychological damage and depression (also a lie).

An abortion doctor in Los Angeles recalls when a patient came to him for a first-trimester abortion with the picture of a sonogram she'd received from a Crisis Pregnancy Center she visited. They told her her fetus was 10 weeks old and gave her a picture of an embryo with arm and leg buds. But when the doctor gave her a sonogram, he found the pregnancy was only five weeks old, with no discernible features whatsoever.[4] They gave this woman a photo of someone else's pregnancy.

Many CPCs model themselves to look like abortion clinics and won't tell pregnant women they don't offer abortion as an option. In 2018, trump's illegitimate Supreme Court[5] ruled CPCs have a First Amendment right to not disclose that they don't offer abortions.

In other words, the First Amendment right to lie.

Why? Why all the cruelty and deception? And why do forced birthers routinely vote against policies and policies that offer real-life tried-and-true ways of reducing abortion numbers?

Here in Kansas, the Catholic church spent whopping $3 million[6] on advertising meant to convince voters to ban abortion, and they failed. That's $3 million that went to deceptive television, internet and radio ads that could've gone to Kansas women and girls who would have kept their pregnancies willingly if they'd just had the resources to do so.

The only other option forced birthers are offering to poor women is adoption, and there are plenty of religious adoption agencies out there that seemingly can't wait to get their hands on babies poor people can't afford to sell them on to richer families.

For those who need to cover up their pregnancy or who want to give away their babies anonymously, conservatives are installing even more baby drop boxes,[7] usually at hospitals or fire stations, where people can give up their infants without fear of prosecution.

I am not against baby drop boxes. Baby drop boxes have meant babies are surrendered safely rather than left in dumpsters to die.

But is this really the best the greatest country in the world can do for poor women and girls who are forced to carry pregnancies to term? Is this the best we can do for women and girls in abusive homes? Tell them to dump their babies in a box and hope for the best?

In a country full of riches and resources where conservatives are determined to take away abortion rights, why can't the alternatives be kinder to women and babies?

I have no answers.

1. Horsley, Scott, "Abortion Limits Carry Economic Cost for Women," NPR, May 23, 2019, https://www.npr.org/2019/05/23/726294656/a-look-at-the-economics-of-ending-a-pregnancy
2. https://www.houstonpregnancyhelpcenter.org/baby-item-list#:~:text=Now%20all%20Pregnancy%20Center%20ministries,Regarding%20used%20baby%20clothes.
3. McFadden, Cynthia, et al, "In Texas, state-funded crisis pregnancy centers gave medical misinformation to NBC News producers seeking counseling," NBC News, June 29, 2022, https://www.nbcnews.com/politics/supreme-court/texas-state-funded-crisis-pregnancy-centers-gave-medical-misinformatio-rcna34883
4. Hamilton, Jessica and Henneberg, Christine, "Op-Ed: Only states can stop antiabortion 'crisis pregnancy centers' from deceiving consumers," Los Angeles Times, June 22, 2022, https://www.latimes.com/opinion/story/2022-06-22/crisis-pregnancy-centers-abortion-deception-regulation
5. Totenberg, Nina & Sara McCammon; Supreme Court Sides With California Anti-Abortion Pregnancy Centers; June 26, 2018, https://www.npr.org/2018/06/26/606427673/supreme-court-sides-with-california-anti-abortion-pregnancy-centers
6. Castle, Amii, "KC Voices: Watching the Catholic Church buy up religious freedom in Kansas," The Pitch KC, July 27, 2022, https://www.thepitchkc.com/kc-voices-watching-the-catholic-church-buy-up-religious-freedom-in-kansas/
7. Goldstein, Dana, "Drop box for babies: Conservatives promote a way to give up newborns anonymously" New York Times, August 6, 2022, https://www.nytimes.com/2022/08/06/us/roe-safe-haven-laws-newborns.html#:~:text=The%20baby%20boxes%20are%20part,abandoning%20or%20even%20killing%20them.

August 15, 2022

Forced Birthers Demand Hand Recount of Blowout Abortion Vote in Kansas

You may have recently heard that in predictably red Kansas, voters overwhelmingly voted against banning or further restricting abortion in Kansas. The vote was split 60–40 in favor of retaining bodily autonomy for Kansans with uteruses, with a lead of over 165,000 votes for those of us who voted NO to making changes to the Kansas Constitution.

But forced-birth fanatics are now calling for a hand recount, because we have entered the age of conservatives refusing to face reality. Per Kansas law, the people requesting the recount will have to pony up a bond to do so — in this case the cost is about $230,000 — and if the vote doesn't go their way, they'll have to give up that money to pay for the recount. If the vote goes in their favor, the state will assume the cost.

Forced birthers are attempting to crowd fund the cost of the recount, but so far, they are nowhere near reaching the amount of money they need by the deadline. As of this moment, they've raised about $35,000, but they're supposed to have the entire amount turned in by the end of today, Monday, Aug. 15. It'll be interesting to see if some forced-birth initiative from somewhere outside of Kansas swoops in and pays the tab by the end of the day.

This ridiculous demand for a recount belies so many things going on with the authoritarian right:

- Denial of reality and facts
- Rabid need to control other people's lives and bodies against their will
- Complete disrespect for women and trans men
- Disregard of the democratic process

But perhaps the most disgusting aspect of this attempt to remove rights from half the population is that forced birthers are willing to sink an additional $230,000 into a campaign they've already wasted five-and-a-half-million dollars on.[1]

How many poor moms and newborns could the church have helped with all that cash?

Further, I — and many other people — am still furious with forced birthers for even daring to put our rights up for a vote on a ballot. The side of freedom and constitutional rights won because we were fighting mad, not to mention terrified, and therefore moved to action.

The women of Kansas don't deserve that. We do not deserve to be targeted that way by our fellow Kansans. No American should have to fear their rights being targeted by another American. It's sick. If forced birthers really want to affect abortion numbers, there are ways to do that without taking away other people's rights.

The next few elections are going to be critical in keeping fascism out of our state and federal government. The fight is far from over.

1. https://kansasreflector.com/2022/07/19/organization-leading-fight-against-abortion-amendment-tops-6-5-million-in-donations/

September 28, 2022

I Don't Care About Your Anti-Abortion Beliefs

I understand your beliefs about abortion are sincere. I understand you find abortion distasteful. Maybe you find it immoral or disgusting. Perhaps you even think it's murder.

Respectfully, I don't care.

You know what I find even more immoral and disgusting? Forced birth. In fact, for me, and many people I know, there's no comparison between abortion and forced birth. Abortion is a right. Forced birth is a gross violation of the rights of an actual, living, breathing, human being who exists in the world.

Some forced birthers try to insist a fertilized egg is a person, deserving not only of equal rights, but rights above and beyond all the rest of us, which is absurd. You'll never convince me a fertilized egg is a person because that is nonsense, and you know it. But let's say for the sake of silly argument a fertilized egg is a person.

Guess what? No other person has the right to someone else's body, organs, or blood. Not without express permission. You can try to insist sex is "permission" for pregnancy, but that's ridiculous. No one expects to become a parent every time they have sex. No one.

Pregnancy is dangerous. Pregnancy can kill the pregnant person at any time, and it can happen very quickly. Pregnancy is always a threat to the life of the pregnant person, and childbirth always causes injuries. Always. Generally, those injuries are permanent. Every woman and girl has the right to protect her health, her body, her life and her future, and you will not take that right away from my kid. Ever.

You can try to shame me and call me every name in the book, but I won't be moved. You can call me a whore, or tell me I'm going to hell, or warn me I'll have to face God someday, but you'll never, ever convince me my daughter should be forced by the state to carry and birth any pregnancy she doesn't want to, for any reason.

You can believe with all your heart and soul a fertilized egg is a person with rights but you'll never convince me of that, no matter how long we argue. (And anyway, I'm pretty sure you understand a fertilized egg isn't a person. If you had to choose between allowing a petri dish of 100 embryos to be flushed down a toilet or be shot in the head, we both know which choice you would make.)

You can rail with every breath in your body until you're dead that little girls who are raped must give birth because abortion is "murder." That's absolute nonsense and you'll never convince me otherwise. (When you allow exceptions for rape, that's also an admission you understand abortion is not murder.)

You are free to worship fertilized eggs and embryos all you want, but you will never convince me I have to do the same.

You can try to make abortion unavailable by making it illegal, but like prohibition, it never works. Abortion never goes away.

All of the above is doubly true if you're anti-abortion and you don't have a uterus, because you don't know what you're talking about. You've never been pregnant, never birthed a baby, never been vaginally raped, never had a miscarriage — never even had a pap smear — so your opinion is moot.

Abortion has always been part of women's culture, since the beginning of time. Women have always kept the knowledge of how to abort pregnancies they didn't have the resources to care for. Abortion is ubiquitous.

Abortion isn't murder. Abortion isn't immoral. Not being born never hurt anybody.

Finally, in case you weren't aware, medication abortion exists now, which can be mailed directly to peoples' homes, where they can abort their pregnancies in peace, away from your prying eyes and perverted fantasies about forcing your hands and will on little girls and grown women.

And there's not a damn thing you can do about it.

November 6, 2022

I'm Sick of Hearing Men Debate Abortion

Let me preface this rant by firmly stating up front: NOT ALL MEN. But there is a not-small, loud, arrogant group of men out there who honestly believe they have every right to discuss and make decisions about a medical procedure, and a medical condition, they themselves can never experience.

Don't get me wrong — I am certainly not happy with forced-birth women, but at least they understand what they're trying to force on other people, if they've been pregnant, anyway. In fact, I highly suspect many forced-birth women have had kids they didn't really want to and they're so mad about it they want to force the same on all of us.

But to listen to men debate a week limit on abortion when none of them have experienced pregnancy, childbirth, miscarriage or rape, let alone abortion — is infuriating. The hubris is gob smacking.

And the guys who like to debate it, will not shut up about it. You would think they have actual uteruses the way they go on, and on, and on, about "taking responsibility" (what about men's responsibility?) and "vetting the men you sleep with" (why are women responsible for men's morality?) and how "Europe bans abortion after 15 weeks." (Which is not only wrong, but a completely different issue in countries that don't try to hinder access to abortion in the first trimester; actually make affordable healthcare and birth control available to their citizens; and ensure paid maternity and paternity leave.)

But what would I know? I'm just a silly lady who's birthed a baby.

The other guy who's infuriating lately is the guy who claims he's "pro-choice," but doesn't understand why women are freaking the fuck out over losing our bodily autonomy. It's just not that big of a deal, these men assure us. It's all hyperbole and over-exaggeration and we all just need to calm down because people really care more about the economy than abortion and if women don't stop making such a big deal out of things then Democrats could lose the midterms.

Then there's the dudes that threaten if we're not nice to them, they won't vote for our bodily autonomy.

With due respect: Go to hell. My daughter's rights over her own body are non-negotiable.

We would never debate whether embryos deserve more rights than men. Women would never seriously debate forced sterilization for men as a method to lower abortion numbers, yet so many men would still vote to force 40 weeks of pregnancy and childbirth on someone they've never met.

I would never vote for any sort of government bodily control over men and neither would any other woman I know, but supposedly us men-hating feminists are such bitches.

What I don't understand is how it's possible for a person to convince themselves so fully that that someone else doesn't want, or need, their rights.

How does that even happen? Especially with an entire gender… how do you convince yourself your daughter, your mother, your girlfriend, your wife—hell your meter maid—doesn't deserve control over her own body, life and future?

The public should never be voting on medical procedures, under any circumstances. Any layperson who believes otherwise is deluding themselves.

November 9, 2022

I'm Ready to Vote on Men's Bodily Autonomy

Recently, I posted a rant about how I was sick of hearing men debate abortion, because I am. What's most irritating to me is the authority with which they do it. Many men speak about abortion as if they have some sort of special insight into the subject when in fact they do not and cannot, even if they do take the time to properly educate themselves on the subject, which the vast majority of the time, they don't.

Of course, this has infuriated some men who have once again told me they have a right to their ridiculous opinions about abortion (true), and they have a right to vote on abortion care (1000% bullshit).

But let's assume for a moment they are correct and it's okay for Americans to vote to restrict other Americans' bodily autonomy.

Cool.

Because I am absolutely ready to begin voting to restrict men's bodily autonomy in order to lower abortion numbers. But that's not all! Restricting men's bodily autonomy would ALSO lower the birthrate, help the environment, save tax money on social programs AND put more criminals in prison.

Ready? Here we go:

Give boys vasectomies

If that sounds too "extreme" or "invasive," vasectomies are nearly 100% effective in preventing pregnancy. Vasectomies are far safer than pregnancy, childbirth, or tubal ligation. In fact, not a single death can be attributed to vasectomy.[1] Vasectomies are now highly reversable, and only a small percentage of men would be infertile later, and isn't that worth stopping the "evils" of abortion?

When those boys get married, their wives can sign off on their vasectomy reversal. Easy peasy.

Preventing unwanted pregnancies in the first place will help curb population growth and cut costs for taxpayers—after all, paying for pregnant poor women and their resulting kids is incredibly expensive.

Arrest and imprison rapists

This might sound like a no-brainer, but in fact if you're a rapist in the US, you have a GREAT chance of getting away with your crime Scott-free. The successful conviction rate for rapes in this country is a lousy 6%.[2]

Sexual assault is the most underreported crime in the country with only 1/3 of sexual assaults being reported to the authorities, and it's easy to see why.

Why bother with an invasive trip to the hospital to have your rape kit collected and go through all the legal rigmarole to watch your rapist face zero consequences anyway?

Speaking of rape kits, this country STILL has a huge backlog of unprocessed rape[3] kits sitting in warehouses, gathering dust, because that's how much we care about women and girls in this culture.

Some people would have you believe this piss-poor prosecution rate is the fault of "lib judges" and "Hollyweird elites," but in fact the highest rates of rapes are in red states[4]:

Alaska — 147 per 100k
Arkansas — 77 per 100k
Michigan — 72 per 100k
South Dakota — 71 per 100k
Nevada — 68 per 100k
Colorado — 65 per 100k
Nebraska — 63 per 100k
New Mexico — 60 per 100k
Oklahoma — 57 per 100k
Montana — 57 per 100k

In fact, the state with the highest total number of rapes is Texas,[5] which, if you will recall, is where Governor Gregg Abbott said this:

"Rape is a crime, and Texas will work tirelessly to make sure we eliminate all rapists from the streets of Texas by aggressively going out and arresting them and prosecuting them and getting them off the streets. So goal no. 1 in the state of Texas is to eliminate rape so that no woman, no person, will be a victim of rape."[6]

Ironically, Abbott said this after signing into law a ban on abortion after six weeks, with no exceptions for rape or incest.

(For transparency's sake, the state with the second highest number of rapes is California, which has the largest population of any state in the Union.)

Many conservatives would have you believe only a small portion of abortions are the result of rape, but these numbers and facts clearly indicate otherwise. Meanwhile in Texas, demand for abortion has stayed the same[6], as has the number of rapes.[7] Though Texas does manage to prosecute a whole 9% of rape cases[8], officials estimate the number of rapes reported in Texas is only 10%. That's right. Ninety percent of rapes go completely unreported in big ol' Texas. Again, can you blame people for not reporting?

It's time to get to work, ladies! We need to vote more women into office and start writing these bills. Clearly men cannot be trusted to control their own bodies when it comes to unplanned pregnancy and rape, so it's time for women to guide them to a more moral place.

1. St Pete Urology, "What is the success rate of vasectomy?" June 4, 2017, https://stpeteurology.com/success-rate-vasectomy/#:~:text=For%20instance%2C%20in%20comparison%20to,same%20number%20of%20tubal%20ligations.
2. Rape, Abuse & Incest National Network (RAINN), "The Criminal Justice System: Statistics", https://www.rainn.org/statistics/criminal-justice-system
3. Rape, Abuse & Incest National Network (RAINN), "Addressing the Rape Kit Backlog", https://www.rainn.org/articles/addressing-rape-kit-backlog
4. https://worldpopulationreview.com/states
5. Stastica.com; "Total number of forcible rape cases reported in the United States in 2020, by state", https://www.statista.com/statistics/232524/forcible-rape-cases-in-the-us-by-state/
6. Weber, Paul & Jamie Stengle, Associated Press, "Texas Vow to 'Eliminate All Rapists' Rings Hollow at Clinics," Sept. 25, 2022, https://www.usnews.com/news/us/articles/2022-09-25/despite-texas-plan-to-end-rape-assault-clinics-remain-busy
7. Mizan, Nusaiba; Austin American Statesman; "Fact-check: Does Texas have highest number of rape offenses in nation?" August 7, 2022, https://www.statesman.com/story/news/politics/politifact/2022/08/07/fact-check-does-texas-have-most-rape-offenses-united-states/65382978007/
8. Gigafact.org; "Are most rapes and sexual assaults in Texas reported and do most perpetrators get arrested? No" Thursday, September 9, 2021, https://gigafact.org/fact-briefs/are-most-rapes-and-sexual-assaults-in-texas-reported-and-do-most-perpetrators-get-arrested

December 1, 2022

The Forced-Birth Baby Market is Here

The New York Times just published a disturbing, well-written article about forced birth and its horrifying consequences in the US. At sixteen years old, Giselle was a girl from a poor, dysfunctional home, who went before a judge to ask for an abortion as a minor without parental permission. She made a point to appear pulled-together, as though she was a good kid who'd made a mistake and wanted to finish high school. She knew she wasn't mature enough to give birth to and raise twins, and she also knew she wasn't going to be able to turn to either of her parents for financial help.

But because she was underage and couldn't count on her mother to approve the abortion, she was forced to appear before a judge to get his permission instead. When asked why she didn't want to choose adoption, she stated that it would be too emotionally difficult to hand away her babies to someone else.

The judge, a 72-year-old white man, decided Giselle was "mature enough" to give birth to her twins. Not having the resources to leave the state for an abortion, Giselle had her babies, and the result is heartbreaking.

The article is long, but well worth the read. It's a detailed example of how absurd it is for judges to have the arbitrary power to make the decision to force a young woman into a financial situation she has no control over, driving her to financial ruin and personal despair. And Giselle isn't the only one suffering now. So are her girls and their father.

At one point, Giselle was working four jobs to try to provide for those babies, and that was with financial help from her boyfriend. Now she's been forced to give them up to a family that's more well-off than she is — which was exactly the nightmare scenario she wanted to avoid.

This dystopian reality where poor people are denied access to abortion care and forced to have children they can't afford doesn't seem to bother the so-called "prolife" movement. Their only concern is the pregnancy is carried to term and birthed. It doesn't matter if poor women can't afford to keep those babies because they can just be sold on to families with more money. (Preferably to well-off white families who vote Republican.)

Conservatives refuse to raise wages or expand the social safety net so that poor people are able to keep those babies, and they're not stepping up with private funds, either. So-called Pregnancy Care Centers give so little financial help to poor mothers as to be laughable, and the people who donate to them would be better served to give that cash directly to a poor mom. Conservatives are not covering the costs of medical bills, or housing, or child care, so that poor moms can either work or stay at home with their newborns. Because, of course, taking care of a newborn is a 24-hour job that must be covered by someone.

Conservatives are literally setting up a legal baby market.

This is not freedom. This is not just. This is a clear, gross violation of constitutional, and human, rights. Four people's lives have now been deeply, inalterably affected on a judge's whim, and not for the better. In fact, the traumatic fallout could affect the four of them for the rest of their lives.

If rightwing politicians were genuine in their desire to reduce abortion numbers they would enact policies that do that — comprehensive sex education in schools, free birth control, affordable healthcare and paid maternity leave.

But listen to their words: They want to save babies.

They don't want to save moms. They don't want to save dads. They don't want to save children.

Just "babies."

January 2, 2023

The Media Must Do Better at Covering Abortion

This week, the New York Times released a (stink)bombshell of an article about the political issue of abortion titled When Does Life Begin?

With the title itself, the article starts off on entirely the wrong premise, and goes through a longwinded, completely unnecessary philosophical debate about when a fertilized egg becomes a person. When it comes to abortion, it doesn't matter when life begins. The only "person" who matters in this equation is the pregnant person. There is already a living, breathing person who exists in the here and now, and only they get to make a decision about whether or not they want to risk their life, health and finances on a pregnancy.

The mainstream media has got to stop centering the abortion issue on the pregnancy, and always, *always* center the issue on the pregnant person. The pregnancy is irrelevant. But that's what the forced-birth movement does — it completely erases any mention of the pregnant person — let alone their rights, and centers the entire abortion argument on a fertilized egg, which is utter nonsense. They have spent many years, and millions (billions?) of dollars pushing a misogynistic fairy tale that somehow pregnancy renders the pregnant person void of all rights.

The media has got to stop letting forced birth extremists control the abortion narrative. This is not a "both sides" issue. It is a human rights violation to force anyone through pregnancy and childbirth, which is body altering, life altering, and dangerous.

I am tired of reading articles in large, mainstream, respected publications that don't bother to do basic fact checking on what their journalists — male and female — write about abortion. They'll fact check any other topic but that one, and I can only surmise it's because so many people assume they know the facts about pregnancy, childbirth and abortion, when in fact they don't.

Mainstream news outlets must stop only interviewing politicians and activists about the issue of abortion and calling it good. Any story about abortion must also include a medical professional's point of view, whether that's an obstetric doctor, nurse, or midwife, and just to be safe, someone with medical expertise should proofread any articles — and opinion pieces — about abortion before they go to press. Abortion coverage should be based in science and medicine, not rhetoric or religious dogma. Lies and inaccuracies should be pointed out and the truth explained. That is literally the job of the news.

The mainstream media largely hasn't bothered to educate the public about abortion facts, which has left an information vacuum extremists have taken full advantage of. Make no mistake: The forced birth political movement is based entirely on lies, and they have worked hard to push deliberate disinformation into the popular consciousness. The rise of social media has made it easy for them to do.

The forced-birth political movement's "greatest hits" include outright lies such as:
- You'll regret your abortion later. (There are documented studies showing this isn't true.)
- Your abortion will cause cancer. (Bullshit.)
- Your abortion will cause depression. (More lies.)
- Abortion hurts women. (It's actually not having access to abortion that hurts women, medically, mentally and financially.)

- It's legal to abort babies up to birth and beyond in the US! (This one is so outrageous you'd think no adult could or would actually believe it, but sadly, millions of Americans have been duped.)

As a journalist myself, I am absolutely fed up with abortion coverage in this country. Journalists must do better.

January 4, 2023

Women and Girls' Bodies are Not Public Property

There is a disturbing, persistent belief among many Americans that women and girls' bodies do not belong to ourselves as men's bodies do. (With the exception of the draft years.) Or, more accurately, that bodies with uteruses are public property to be poked, prodded, invaded, debated, impregnated and regulated. (I did not mean to sound like Al Sharpton, I swear.)

When I say this, I'm not just talking about abortion bans and forced birth. I'm talking about pregnancy and rape and the guy who grabs your ass at the grocery store — all of it. All of it contributes to a false sense of entitlement to female bodies. When I was birthing my daughter, no fewer than a dozen people wandered in and out of the room all night long, as I lay there, spread eagle, with nothing more than a hospital gown sort of thrown over my midsection. Occasionally a boob would slip out and I'd try to cover it back up, but it didn't matter. Once my daughter was born, the nurses would walk up to me, whip open my gown, grab a boob and stuff it in my daughter's mouth. "Like this!" they'd say, as if *I* were the baby.

I got over my shyness pretty quick that night, and I understand medical people have seen the insides and outsides of all kinds of bodies. Still, the feeling that I was a puerile medical curiosity to behold, as opposed to a scared woman birthing her first child, was palpable.

This belief that female bodies are public property is held by both men and women, and recently, it has come to the attention of our corporate and Christo-fascist Overlords that Americans are having fewer and fewer babies.

The reason, of course, that Americans are having fewer and fewer babies is purely financial. We simply cannot afford to have kids, what with skyrocketing housing, food, and medical costs, and salaries that haven't kept pace with inflation.

This is a problem the Overlords could fix in an instant by raising salaries, providing medical insurance and more social safety nets. If people felt secure enough to do so, they'd start popping out babies. But the Overlords don't want to share their unearned hoards of wealth, because they are greedy, immoral jerks. Instead, they've opted for direct control of uterine-bearing bodies by successfully banning abortion in several states. The result, of course, has already been a nightmare parade of disgusting medical atrocities American women of childbearing age have already had to endure post-Roe V Wade.

We're already hearing stories of women being forced to wait at home with sepsis until they are near dead to be deemed "sick enough" to be granted life-saving abortions. A woman in Louisiana was forced to go through hours of physical and mental agony giving birth to her dead baby because of the abortion ban there. Another Louisiana woman had to leave the state to abort the skull-less fetus she was carrying that would die soon after birth. Little girls are being forced to travel out of state for abortion care, because unfortunately, the rape and impregnation of little girls in the US is far more prevalent than any of us want to talk about or admit.

Women fighting cancer are being denied lifesaving drugs because those drugs cause abortion, and pregnant women who discover after the fact they have cancer are being denied abortions and cancer treatment. Women who have autoimmune diseases and gastric ulcers are having trouble getting the drugs they need to manage their conditions because those drugs are abortion inducing.

There is an army of rabid forced birthers out there willing and ready to help enable this dangerous takeover of our daughter's bodies. My daughter now has fewer rights over her own body than I did during my childbearing years. Some forced birthers are even taking steps to try to limit access to birth control.

It's an obscene, direct attack on our own citizens.

Women and girls and trans men do not lose all rights to our own bodies because we are pregnant. There is no factual, rational argument to make abortion illegal. In fact, the opposite is true. Maternal and infant deaths go up in states that ban abortion. That is a fact.

The idea that a fertilized egg has more rights than a born person is a religious construct that a majority of us do not share. Even the current Illegitimate Supreme Court refused to weigh in on fetal personhood, because they know it's nonsense, legally and otherwise. Keeping abortion legal doesn't impact anyone's rights — those who believe fertilized eggs are sacred are free to continue to believe that, and they're still try to convince the rest of us their view is correct. They are also free to pump out as many babies as they wish and us heathens won't try to stop them.

Finally, most of us don't believe we need more people, here in the 'States or anywhere. Most of us believe there are in fact too many people on the planet, and if we continue the rapid population explosion of our species, we're putting the entire human race in jeopardy.

The only people who benefit from more people — more politically disenfranchised, underpaid people without adequate medical care, are the Overlords themselves, who can afford to shield themselves from adverse weather events, food and water shortages, and even attacks from us peasants.

If they can make women's bodies public property, they can make men's bodies public property too. We must ensure every American has the right to bodily autonomy.

Feb 28, 2023

Yes, Jessa Duggar Had an Abortion

Chaos erupted in the "prolife" community this week when it was announced that reality television show star and outspoken proponent of forced birth, Jessa Duggar Seewald of 19 Kids and Counting fame, revealed she had a D&C over the holidays to remove a problem pregnancy.

There seems to be confusion over whether or not the fetus had actually died — forced birthers insist Jessa has reported there was no heartbeat, but news stories have so far only reported that the ultrasound technician said: 'The sac looks good. The baby does not.'

Whether or not the fetus had a heartbeat is irrelevant. What's important is the fetus had some sort of fatal anomaly and would not have survived outside the uterus. In either case, the pregnant person has a right to appropriate treatment, which is removal of the pregnancy, if they so wish.

Somehow Jessa was able to be immediately admitted for a dilation and curettage procedure (more commonly known as D&C or D&E) to remove the pregnancy, despite the fact she hails from Arkansas, which has a total ban on abortion. By the wording of Arkansas' own law, Jessa's procedure appears to have been performed illegally, because the only exception Arkansas allows for abortion is a threat to the mother's life, and Jessa's life was clearly not in immediate danger.

Meanwhile, women in the exact same medical situation as Jessa are being turned away from hospitals to wait at home until they either pass the fetus via spontaneous abortion (miscarriage) or become sick enough to warrant an abortion to save their lives.

But forced birthers are furious that many people are correctly pointing out that the procedure Jessa was able to obtain — whether or not the fetus was still alive — was an ABORTION.

Therein lies the problem with laypeople trying to make laws about a medical procedure. They are operating with a different vocabulary than the legal and medical fields. Hospitals that perform D&Cs to remove a miscarriage call that procedure an abortion.

REMOVING A DEAD BABY IS NOT AN ABORTION forced birthers insist, and boy are they *pissed* about people using that word. But in the medical field, the procedure is an abortion, whether the fetus is living or not. In fact, miscarriage treatment is usually listed as an abortion on the hospital bill. "Prolifers" are not having it. They all seem to think abortion is a black-and-white issue that's easy to navigate, but that's because they are not doctors. They don't see all the nuances and bizarre complications that can happen in a pregnancy. This is why abortion should always be a decision made between patient and doctor. Period.

The real tragedy is this result of average women losing the right to a D&C for a miscarriage or a dead fetus because of abortion bans was entirely predictable. The entire reason Roe was passed in the first place was because doctors were tired of not being able to treat, and save, their patients.

Before Roe was passed, Hollywood actress Debbie Reynolds, mother of Carrie Fisher, was forced to carry around a dead fetus in her uterus for two entire months when it died inside her at only 7 months. She was forced to carry the pregnancy to term and deliver a stillborn baby.

Reynolds had this to say about the experience:

"It was a very hard thing to get over because, in those days, there were no abortions allowed, whether you were ill or whether you were raped or whether the child died," she remarked. "Which is disgusting to think that there (are) those laws."

The treatment for miscarriage, or electively ending a live pregnancy, are exactly the same, which is why doctors are reluctant to treat their patients when states ban abortion. Any forced birther at any time could take a doctor to court over treating a miscarriage, insisting it was illegal. If the jury agrees, the doctor loses their license, or worse, ends up in prison. If you haven't noticed, forced birthers tend to not be reasonable people, and any chance to put a "baby killing" doctor in prison would be an absolute dream come true for some of them.

But what about exceptions to abortion bans? Well, as I mentioned earlier, there are some states — like Arkansas and Louisiana — that have banned abortion only if the pregnancy is a threat to the mother's life. If the fetus dies in utero, and isn't expelled, and the mother's life isn't in immediate danger, some hospitals are turning away patients who then have to wait until they are starting to become septic to be treated.

There are also women with unviable pregnancies being denied abortion care, like this woman who had to leave Louisiana to have her fetus aborted. The fetus was alive but developing without a skull.

Interestingly, "prolifers" are divided on cases like these — some think an abortion is not only warranted, but don't understand why doctors in states with full abortion bans aren't immediately aborting those pregnancies. But the other half of the "prolife" crowd says it's murderous evil to kill such a fetus, and it's God's will that a woman carry the pregnancy to term and birth the baby, even if it means the baby will suffer before it dies.

It's this grey area that has doctors in a legal bind. What if they perform an abortion on a technically living fetus that's doomed to die, some forced birther takes them to court, and the judge is also conservative? They'll go to prison, that's what. Even when exceptions are written into abortion laws, doctors carry the burden of proof that they followed the law to the letter.

This is happening in the US, right now, in states with full abortion bans. "Prolifers" insist doctors aren't following the law by turning such women away. Lawyers say they absolutely are.

Pregnant people are paying the price.

March 4, 2023

Stop Romanticizing Pregnancy and Childbirth

There is a disturbing culture of minimizing the dangers of pregnancy and childbirth in the United States. That would be bad enough on its own if it wasn't also for the fact that many people refuse to acknowledge pregnancy and childbirth:

- kills approximately 800 American women every single year, and that statistic has stalled
- causes lasting, sometimes severe injuries
- quite often does not go smoothly
- increases a woman's chance of being murdered by her intimate partner

Some of this culture of idealizing pregnancy and childbirth is because women are trained to keep quiet about our bodily functions and body parts because they're viewed as disgusting. Women will swap birth war stories when we're with each other, but almost never in mixed company, so as to not gross anyone out or, God forbid, make a man uncomfortable.

We don't talk about our perineums routinely being torn and having to be sewn up. I have a friend who had a fourth degree tear that later became infected. She was in agonizing pain for months.

We don't talk about the incontinence childbirth can cause — and that's both bladder and/or bowel incontinence — because who wants to hear that?

We don't talk about vaginal prolapse, which is when all of that pushing and straining through birth causes the pelvic floor muscles and tendons to stretch so badly that the top of the vagina begins to collapse into itself and falls into the vaginal canal. Definitely not a topic for dinner conversation.

Much of this romanticization of pregnancy and childbirth is the fault of religion, which views babies as "gifts from God," and how can that possibly be bad? Of course, there's that whole "suffering for Eve's sins," business. That's fine if that's what you believe, but it's certainly not what I believe.

Human pregnancy and childbirth is not dangerous because it's a punishment for Eve's sins. It's because 1) humans walk on two legs instead of four, which means a smaller-than-normal pelvic opening as compared to most mammals, and 2) we have large brains, which means large skulls, which makes having babies more dangerous for humans than other mammals. The evolutionary tradeoff is that the humans who survive gestation and birth are far smarter than your average mammal, even though our pregnancies are more dangerous, for both mother and baby.

Then there are the multitude of other health complications of pregnancy, which happen far more often than we like to admit: miscarriage, infection, pre-eclampsia (a type of deadly high blood pressure in pregnancy which can appear seemingly out of nowhere and kill quickly), gestational diabetes, fetuses with fatal deformities that won't survive birth, and on and on.

Yet the glossing over of the real dangers of pregnancy and childbirth persist. There's the pervasive myth that because pregnancy and childbirth are "natural" they are safe. The fact of the matter is pregnancy can put a huge amount of stress on all of the mother's vital organs, especially the kidneys, liver and heart, and even the brain. Many things that are "natural" are dangerous or deadly: venomous snakes, bears, radiation, arsenic, etc.

The American denial of the huge toll pregnancy and childbirth can take on a woman, girl, or trans man's body is so severe we don't even mandate paid time off from work to recover after childbirth. This is, in my opinion, hugely disrespectful to half the population.

How do women respond? We deal with it, and we don't complain out loud, because we've been trained not to. Unfortunately, this seems to only perpetuate the myth that pregnancy and childbirth are "natural" and virtually trouble-free.

Self defense for me, but not thee

Many people in the US will look you straight in the face and declare they have the right to shoot and kill an intruder on their property, and in the very next breath declare that women and girls have no right to protect their lives, bodies, finances and futures from a fertilized egg.

The only justification for this sort of skewed sense of bodily autonomy is pure misogyny — and yes, there are millions of women helping to hold up that system of belief. There is a very strong tradition in this country that men's bodies belong to them, while women and girls' bodies are pretty much public property to be regulated. But this is no longer the 1800s, or even the 1900s, and it's time women have ownership of our own bodies.

July 14, 2023

The 'Culture of Life' is Also a Culture of Shame & Trauma

In 2012, a class-action lawsuit was brought against the Canadian Government for all the coerced adoptions of babies of single and teen moms from 1940 to 1990. Plaintiffs were able to bring the lawsuit against the government because taxpayer dollars were funneled into maternity homes for unwed mothers, which were usually run by churches.

As this was going on in Canada, American broadcast journalist Dan Rather began looking into the broad phenomenon of coerced adoptions that occurred all across Europe, the US, Australia and Canada, and he found a similar pattern. The white, Western culture from post-World War II up until about the early 1990s was the same: Shame white girls for getting pregnant out of wedlock, send them away to a maternity home, take their babies from them immediately or soon after birth, and adopt those babies to married couples.

He called the piece *Adopted or abducted? Veil of secrecy lifts slowly on decades of forced adoptions for unwed mothers around the globe.*

Rather details how most of those girls were flat-out lied to and told they weren't legally allowed to keep their babies. While they stayed in those maternity homes waiting to give birth, they were often openly bullied and shamed by staff, and reminded again and again they wouldn't be keeping their babies because they were moral failures. Often girls were made to give birth without pain killers and in the most humiliating settings possible. Some were never even allowed to see their babies before the babies were whisked away and adopted out to families.

Black and Hispanic girls, on the other hand, were encouraged to keep their babies, as they were considered to be more promiscuous and have lower moral standards anyway.

Though the Catholic Church ran the majority of the maternity homes and adoption agencies throughout the Western world, in reality, the entire Western culture supported this arrangement — churches of all faiths, hospitals, parents, schools, governments — girls were supposed to feel shame for getting pregnant out of wedlock, as was their family. The only way to mitigate that public shame was to send bad girls away, and remove the evidence of their moral failings by giving away the babies and never speaking of their existence again.

To be sure, this is one way to handle teen pregnancy. But the real-life fallout was emotionally devastating, for both the moms and their kids. (And presumably, many of the dads, as well.)

In the book, *The Girls Who Went Away: The Hidden History of Women Who Surrendered Children for Adoption in the Decades Before Roe v. Wade*, author Ann Fessler interviews the women who were forced to give up their babies, finally giving voice to their pain. As an adoptee herself, separated from her mother, Fessler wanted these powerful, painful stories to be told.

One British woman, who is now in her seventies and whose child was taken from her in 1964 had this to say: "I, and thousands of women like me, were coerced into giving up our children. I was a perfectly healthy, capable adult. I'm still angry my child was taken away."

In 2018, Canada released a report on coerced adoptions called "The Shame is Ours," detailing the trauma caused to 300,000 Canadian women by taking their babies away from them. Canada and the State of Western Australia issued formal apologies to the women whose babies had been taken.

The Washington Post did a great exposé on U.S. District Judge Matthew Kacsmaryk, the judge who, in April of 2023, placed an injunction on the FDA approval for the abortion drug mifepristone, which had previously been legal for 20 years. (Mifepristone is also used to treat Cushing Syndrome.)

The WaPo article detailed how Kacsmaryk's judicial decision was based entirely on his Christian beliefs and upbringing:

"Matthew Kacsmaryk was a 22-year-old law student when he drove to a small city in west Texas to spend a day with a baby he would probably never see again.

"He was in Abilene to support his sister, who, pregnant at 17, had fled to a faraway maternity home to avoid the scorn she feared from their Christian community. But holding his nephew in his arms — then leaving the baby with adoptive parents — also solidified Kacsmaryk's belief that every pregnancy should be treasured, his sister recalled, even those that don't fit neatly into a family's future plans."

By all accounts, Kacsmaryk's family — including his sister who had to give up her baby — are still very happy with the decision they made, and in fact, clearly believe it was the correct decision. They believe in it so much, they apparently want all girls and women to once again be shamed for unwanted pregnancies and suffer the consequences of their actions, with no option to abort.

To be sure, in the years after Roe Vs. Wade was passed, abortions went up, dramatically. But by 1998, abortion numbers were back down to pre-Roe levels, and that was with an increasing population. Why? Because of sex education in public schools and easier access to birth control. The AIDS crisis also taught lots of Americans to get serious about using condoms.

The irony is very real: Just as we, as a culture and society, were starting to unpack and face the trauma caused by all those forced adoptions, Roe Vs. Wade is overturned here in the US. But we Americans have shockingly short memories, and the flood of disinformation in the last decade hasn't helped anything.

The Dobbs decision has definitely resulted in some forced births, and will ultimately result in some forced adoptions — not because of shame, necessarily, but because of economics, especially as the wealth gap in the US continues to widen. The glee with which the antichoice crowd has embraced the return of the punishment of forced pregnancy and childbirth is truly heartbreaking. Republican politicians are now throwing millions of dollars at Crisis Pregnancy Centers in a smokescreen of offering "help" to poor, pregnant women and girls, but in true fashion, mostly what the Crisis Pregnancy Centers do is offer up lots of lies, guilt and shame, but no real financial support.

That's where they want to take us. This isn't just about controlling women and girls, and it's certainly not about "saving babies"— it's about bringing back a barbaric, hurtful ideology, and forcing it on all of us

How to Be a Middle-Aged Dork

July 8, 2023

Recently, I had occasion to attend an all-day retreat in a corporate building in downtown Kansas City with the abortion fund I volunteer for. One of our board members had access to the building, and even I have to admit their conference room ended up being a great space for us to use for the day.

Suffice to say, I hadn't been in a real, honest-to-God corporate building in a long damn time, and I'm now getting to the age that new technology sort of takes me off guard — occasionally — but whatever. I'm trying to roll with it. When we arrived, we had to check in with the front desk crew who confirmed we were allowed to be in the building, and which floor we were going to, for security reasons. They then programmed in the floor we needed to get to because, much to my surprise when we entered one of the six elevators, there were NO BUTTONS. Passengers literally cannot operate the lift themselves.

So cool, fine, whatevs, we get up to the 22nd floor and we start our all-day retreat. We take a break at noon for lunch, and because I despise corporate culture and also I'm just fucking nosy, after lunch I decided to wander around our floor. I didn't touch anything — I just looked. Eventually, I came across a door marked "Stairs," and decided to duck in there.

Why would a grown-ass woman behave this way? Because in my head, I'm still twelve years old. When we were kids, our dad would often take my brother and me to work with him at the university where he was a professor, and then ignore us. My brother and I had endless adventures wandering through buildings, upstairs and down, through long, dark empty hallways and into classrooms and conference halls exploring, and it was fun.

I stepped into the stairwell, the door clicked shut behind me and I thought, jokingly, I hope that door didn't just lock behind me... surely not.

Just to make sure I could get back to our conference room, I turned around, tried the door, and it was locked. No worries, I thought. It's probably just this floor they keep locked. I went up a flight and tried that door. Locked. I went down to the 21st floor but wasn't surprised that when I checked that door, it was also locked.

Suddenly, I remembered it's the modern age and we are all tethered to a smart phone! I could just call for help! My heart dropped when I patted my pockets, only to discover I'd left my cell phone lying on the conference table, which was odd because I'm thoroughly addicted to my phone. (A friend pointed out to me later that my cell phone likely wouldn't have worked in the concrete-encased stairwell, anyway.)

That's when I realized I was going to have to run down 22 flights of stairs, tell the nice ladies at the front desk I had locked myself out of the 22nd floor, and ask them if they'd pretty please send me back up. (They were very kind, and didn't even laugh at me too much.)

Running DOWN 22 flights of stairs is no bigs, right? It used to be no bigs. After all, there's a huge gravity assist. Turns out at age 51, running down 21 flights of stairs isolates your quads like a MOTHERFUCKER and then you feel like you've got useless, stretched-out, painful rubber band thighs for the next three days.

I made all the way down the stairs, back up the elevator and into the conference room JUST as the meeting was resuming, little droplets of sweat dripping down my neck.

No one was the wiser. I hope.

Author's Note

Most, but not all, of the essays found in this collection were originally published on my blog at Medium.com, which lives at medium.com/@amberbobamber-43268, but you can just go to Medium.com and search for Amber Fraley. In addition to more carefully written essays, I post my rants, mostly about recent political events. There are also many other fantastic writers on the site, and if you've thought about blogging yourself, I recommend it! The formatting is attractive, the site is user-friendly, and Medium has made a commitment to supporting real humans as opposed to AI content. (No, they didn't pay me to say that, but I reserve the right to retract it all should they suddenly become unconscionable assholes.)

You can be sure my abortion commentary will be ongoing there until these barbaric, discriminatory abortion bans end. That story isn't finished, not by a long shot. And yes, I am aware that "trump" isn't capitalized anywhere in this book, because I am that petty bitch.

About the Author

AMBER FRALEY IS YOUR TYPICAL GEN XER suburban Kansas wife and mom of one who grew up a book nerd in a dysfunctional family and now writes about those experiences as hilarious therapy. She's the author of the darkly humorous essay collection *From Kansas, Not Dorothy*, and the viral essay *Gen X Will Not Go Quietly*, as well as numerous human interest articles in regional magazines. Growing up in Lawrence and Wichita, Amber spent her formative years with her face in a book or at the mall with her friends. She loves the Kansas with all her heart, is frequently awkward in public, and desperately wishes to see a tornado and live to tell the tale.

Follow her on Facebook, read her public blog on Medium.com or visit her website at https://www.amberfraley.com/

Other BOOKS you might enjoy FROM Anamcara Press LLC

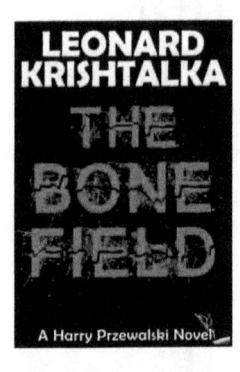

LEONARD KRISHTALKA — THE BONE FIELD
A Harry Przewalski Novel
ISBN: 9781941237-33-5
$18.99

LEONARD KRISHTALKA — DEATH SPOKE
A Harry Przewalski Novel
ISBN: 9781941237-30-4
$18.99

LEONARD KRISHTALKA — THE CAMEL DRIVER
A Harry Przewalski Novel
ISBN: 9781941237-32-8
$18.95

A PARTING GLASS — a novel
Tess Banion
ISBN: 9781941237-13-7
$18.95

SEARCHING FOR SPENSER
NIEA WINNER — NATIONAL INDIE EXCELLENCE AWARDS
Margaret Kramar
ISBN: 9781941237-18-2
$16.95

PHOTOGRAPHER PARATROOPER POW — A Wyoming Cowboy in Hitler's Germany
M. Carroll
ISBN: 9781941237-08-3
$24.95

Available wherever books are sold and at:
anamcara-press.com

Thank you for being a reader! Anamcara Press publishes select works and brings writers & artists together in collaborations in order to serve community and the planet.
Your comments are always welcome!

Anamcara Press
anamcara-press.com